THE ART AND MAKING OF
PREACHER

THE ART AND MAKING OF PREACHER

ISBN: 9781785655883

Published by
Titan Books
A division of Titan Publishing Group Ltd
144 Southwark St
London
SE1 0UP

WWW.TITANBOOKS.COM

First edition: 2018

10 9 8 7 6 5 4 3 2 1

To receive advance information, news, competitions,
and exclusive offers online, please sign up for the Titan
newsletter on our website: www.titanbooks.com

Did you enjoy this book? We love to hear from our readers.
Please e-mail us at: readerfeedback@titanemail.com or
write to Reader Feedback at the above address.

A CIP catalogue record for this title is available from the
British Library.

Printed and bound in China.

Paul Davies worked in journalism for twenty-five years.
He is now a freelance writer, and creative consultant.

THE ART AND MAKING OF

PREACHER

PAUL DAVIES

TITAN BOOKS

CONTENTS

FOREWORD

SETH ROGEN AND EVAN GOLDBERG

Seth: We started reading *Preacher* in high school.

Evan: My brother had read it and was like, "You GOTTA check this shit out! It's fucking crazy." I read it immediately and dear god, it was fucking crazy.

Seth: And then Evan came to me and was like, "You gotta read this shit. It's fucking crazy." And I did, and it was, in fact, fucking crazy. Garth Ennis and Steve Dillon had created our favorite thing ever.

Evan: A thing we would tonally rip off for years and years to come.

Seth: Don't say that. We'll get sued. Just keep going.

Evan: About three years later Seth moved to LA, and about eight years after that we had enough sway to try to attach ourselves to our favorite comic books.

Seth: Unfortunately, nobody would attach us to *Preacher* because much more talented people kept being more interested in making it.

Evan: Lucky for us, although those people were more talented than us, they weren't more fucked up than us, and therefore they were unable to truly bring *Preacher* to life.

Seth: Eventually, after every single person in Hollywood who was more talented than us failed, the project landed in our laps. We found Sam Catlin, who at the time was living under a bridge near a swamp.

Evan: Yeah, Sam was doing this thing where he lived under a bridge and if you wanted to pass over the bridge, you had to answer like two riddles.

Seth: It was three riddles.

Evan: Oh yeah, three riddles. Anyway, we answered his riddles and he came on board to run the show.

Seth: We found the greatest cast in the world, and they got to be directed by the greatest directors in the world.

Evan: That's fucking right they did.

Seth: Bringing the show to life has been a great joy. We get to deal with Drama, Comedy, Action, Horror, Sci-fi, and some light but effective Eroticism.

Evan: We got to make *Preacher*, and to us, that's just fucking fantastic.

INTRODUCTION

I would like to confess something. There have been moments during *Preacher* that I have reconsidered my own path in life. I've thought about family. I've looked into my own soul. Watching *Preacher* has changed me. This is God's honest truth. If that still means anything.

Exploring the world of AMC's *Preacher*, learning from the production team and the cast, and creator/writer Garth Ennis, there

is a sense that the show is something unusually important. There is something special about it. This book endeavors to shed light on what that means.

Certainly, one of the most exciting points to consider is how *Preacher* entered production in the first place. Essentially that, even until very recently, such a challenging concept found it difficult to get past the managing bodies of traditional broadcasters. As Ennis contemplates, "I would say that it might be that TV executives are now more ready for *Preacher* than they were ten years ago. We did bounce off a couple of places where some of the guys liked it and a lot of people didn't. Now it seems that there is greater acceptance."

The artists assembled to bring Ennis' twisted and nuanced "movie America" to life are each exceptionally gifted in their own right. Individual contributors have had freedom to shape the transition of *Preacher* from comic book to live-action drama, playing to producers Evan Goldberg and Seth Rogen's strength of capturing the vitality of improvisation within a very tightly directed environment. This includes everybody, from central relationships formed between Jesse, Tulip and Cassidy, through performances from the youngest cast members, and practical effects design that makes the supernatural element

so horribly convincing.

Watching how his creation was developed and built upon was interesting for Garth Ennis, and received his stamp of approval: "I liked seeing Jesse struggling with his role as a small town preacher, which was something we didn't do much with in the book. Trying to be a good guy, wary of slipping back into his old ways. Watching him demolish the assholes in the bar, way back in the first episode was a lot of fun. And the way in which the two angels were developed was very good — particularly Fiore and his new life in show business." Without a doubt, so much of what pops in *Preacher* is due to the casting agents' keen eye, married with tremendously thoughtful costume design, and then every idiosyncratic twitch and wardrobe stitch lavishly observed through some of the world's best cinematographers.

"There's something about *Preacher* that has a nostalgic feel," explains executive producer and showrunner Sam Catlin. "Garth always says *Preacher* is a 'foreigner's look at America through American pop culture.' There's a sentimentality about America, both for the good and for the bad. Obviously it takes place in a version of present-day, but it's an 'olden times' version of it. Bill Pope really

set the tone for that, and John Grillo/Andrew Voegeli, our current directors of photography, have done everything they can to meet that standard and take it further. The look of *Preacher* is something we're all proud of. It looks like a movie we had twenty-five days to shoot."

Ennis is thoughtful when asked about what inspired him to write *Preacher* all those years ago: "There was no main element, rather a collection of disparate ones. Examples would be the western movies I'd watched since I was a kid, a good chunk of American crime and horror fiction, my own travels in the US, my interest in the history of the country."

In terms of why Goldberg and Rogen took interest in *Preacher* in the first place, Goldberg says it was because, "Everyone who's read it says, 'This is the craziest thing I've ever seen.' There's a lot of great stories, and they are all very crazy. *The Lord of the Rings* has great scope and is, like, 'the greatest story ever told' and so on. But *Preacher* is just bonkers. You read it, and you can't believe a human sat down with pen to paper and thought these thoughts and scribed

them out and actually convinced somebody to publish it in a book."

When asked to outline what first attracted him to the project, Catlin gamely discloses, "The impossibility of it. When Seth and Evan first gave me Garth's comic I looked at it and said, 'I haven't seen anything like that either in a comic or on a TV show.' So the fact that we were going to have an opportunity to at least try to bring Garth's unbelievable scope, weirdness, and violence to TV was an exciting challenge."

That *Preacher* now spans two seasons provides new inspiration. As Catlin goes on to explain: "The whole show is evolving. For each season we're discovering more and more what the stories are that we want to tell, and how to best tell them. What are the mistakes we've made? How do we make new ones? I think all areas — the directing, acting, and writing — they just keep getting better and better.

"We have Garth's story: a very simple beginning and a very simple ending. Starts with Jesse knowing that God's missing and that he's gotta find him. And then when Jesse finds him he holds him to account. So that's our structure, what we build it all on top of. In

terms of the story arcs, we look at the different worlds we dive into. Season 1, Annville: this west Texas town where Jesse grew up. Season 2: we start to get into the world of New Orleans and the grail and the Saint of Killers. Season 3: we knew we wanted to get into Angelville.

"Yes, there are other worlds we want to expand into going forward, it's just a question of where do we stop along the road first and how many stops along the road can we have before we reach our final destination. And…that's how it works."

Commenting on what originally attracted her to the starring role of Tulip, actress Ruth Negga says, "That supernatural, fantasy, comic book world, I really like and it makes a lot more sense than the average hospital drama. The rules are

sort of broken, you can bend people's ideas of what can be allowed on camera."

"It's the jumble of all the things I grew up relishing, desiring and wanting to watch," says Dominic Cooper, who plays Jesse Custer. "I think it's got something very special about it."

"In essence, it's a Western," details Ennis. "So you have to have this incredible countryside. You have to have these huge desert skies. You have to have sunsets for people to ride off into. The characters themselves have to be giants, have to be archetypes. And I think that's what we're getting [in the show].

"One of the overarching themes is ultimately what a bad idea God is in the first place. You know, how we would be better off just throwing the idea away. I like the thought that the show will take from the comic the notion of heroism — perhaps not pure, slightly battered — against unspeakable villainy. That very American movie feeling of doing the right thing, even if it's at the last minute and you're hanging on by your fingernails doing the right thing."

Remarkably, although purposefully respecting such Hollywood tropes, *Preacher* avoids ever retracing such worn out schemes. It is never corny; even at the pinnacle of crazy, scenes are played smart and captured in a very distinct, splendidly textured style.

As Catlin says, "It has a lot of fun elements to it, including the violence, but the show really is a drama. The characters of *Preacher* are very troubled. The more we get to know them, we understand how damaged they are, how violent they are, how restless they are. They take the stakes of this world very seriously. It's also really silly, perverted and subversive."

British actors perform many of the key roles in *Preacher*, although this is hard to tell just by watching the show. However, behind the scenes, the fact that Ennis is also from the UK meant that his characters were not originally conceived as comic book superheroes. This distinction adds a further, curious layer to the feel of the show, in which even the most mysterious heroes and villains are quite tenderly humanized.

Comments Seth Rogen, "You just don't know what to expect, and that's what was so great with the comic. It was scary, gross, funny and enthralling and emotional and sad... To try to build a show that could support all that was something that we talked a lot about."

AMC's *Preacher* has become as challenging and darkly compelling as the original books from Ennis. Although new characters have been introduced, and the lives of existing ones embellished in many ways, it remains true to Ennis' original intention. The author has been as captivated by the results as the audience.

"Seeing the characters just walking around and interacting is absolutely terrific," says Ennis. "Watching Jesse give his sermons, seeing Cassidy lying in a pool of his own guts, cursing and spitting and trying to escape from his ghastly circumstances.

"I knew that they were gonna have to expand on what I'd done, because there simply isn't enough material in the comic to give them what they want. And I like that they've gone into Annville, to expand the personalities and create some new ones. At the end of the day, I wrote *Preacher* twenty years ago, and it's existed in its comic form for the past fifteen.

"For me, it's very, very interesting to see somebody else come along and approach it from a different tack."

ABOVE: Jesse's life as a preacher is interrupted by two arrivals: an old flame and an old vampire.

From the earliest table reading to the prospect of another season, talk among the team has been of an uncommon group dynamic. From Catlin's point of view as showrunner, the chance to work with Goldberg and Rogen has been as inspirational as it has been wild.

"I did not know Seth and Evan personally, only from their films and brand. They've been amazing collaborators. Both are super smart, excellent producers and directors who are wonderful with story," says Catlin. "I don't know how they do it, but both are extremely organized. Although they're huge fans of the comic, they've known from the outset that what works in most places in the comic might not work on screen. So they were smart in the sense that they didn't let their experience with the comic color what would be best for a cable TV show."

Most fans would agree that casting is perfect for *Preacher*, something Catlin says was "a long process." He continues: "Seth, Evan and I casted during pilot season so we had a tough time finding people. Then, when we did find Joe, Ruth and Dom there weren't any second choices. We just knew Ruth Negga was going to be Tulip, Dominic Cooper was going to be Jesse and Joe Gilgun is Cassidy. We've never looked back from that; they're obviously the heart and soul of the show."

Rogen also expressed how satisfied he has been with the lead roles. "Ruth's incredible. We keep going to give her notes, like, 'Your character should fidget and stuff', then we watch and she does fidget all the time. She seems naturally born for the role. She's really versatile, nailed the accent really quick.

"Dominic's great. His character is the hardest thing, because he's like a Clint Eastwood kind of cowboy. The more we do [with him] the more we realize, 'You only get to say ten words every twenty minutes, you'd better say them really well and make them awesome.' Instead of our normal improvisation shtick, we're working with him constantly and Sam Catlin, honing every line, and asking how do you make a line tell more than the line is."

Catlin confides that one of the reasons he sometimes prefers shooting quieter scenes is because the show has such amazing actors. He references the challenge met by Goldberg and Rogen, adapting their celebrated improvisational style and writing on the moment.

"I wasn't disappointed in terms of how big a show it is: how much it takes to produce and the challenges of getting the right tone, the fights, the blood, the comedy, the drama…" Catlin reflects. "I don't think any of us thought we knew exactly what we were doing, which is what you would expect on a show you hadn't seen before. I think we were all pleasantly surprised by how all the different tones and genres and styles that exist in Garth and Steve Dillon's graphic novel can, if done well, co-exist in one TV show. We thought there may be a good reason why there'd never been a show like this, so it's been very rewarding to see that it works."

JESSE CUSTER

LONDON BORN DOMINIC Cooper has portrayed his fair share of stiff-upper-lipped period drama gentlemen. But for his starring role in *Preacher*, something rather the opposite was required. It helped that Cooper had previously worked with co-star Ruth Negga (Tulip) on the movie *Warcraft: The Beginning* (2016).

For director Evan Goldberg, Dominic was quite the revelation as Jesse Custer. Evan had taken something of a risk by hiring the actor based on his reputation. "We have never, ever just offered somebody a role, especially a role this important," Goldberg admitted. "It was thrilling to find out that Dominic did it better than we could ever have hoped, and is one of the greatest actors I have ever worked with. And more than any actor, you can see him slowly honing in on it, and getting better and better. Literally every take he gets is better than the one before. The only reason he doesn't keep getting better is because we run out of time."

Cooper has also impressed Garth Ennis, the creator and writer of the *Preacher* comic series (on which the TV show is based). "I think Dominic is spot on," he says. "It helps that he looks just like him, but even beyond that he's absolutely nailed the character — that sort of weary hang-dog approach. He's not quite beaten, but he's getting there. Yet within him there's the foundation for the resurgence of the character that will come."

Cooper's distinctly thoughtful, exploratory approach — heck, we might as well call it soul-searching in this case — dovetails neatly with the scriptwriters and producers who all have suggestions to make, often on the fly. Says Cooper, "There are so many different ideas, and different ways in which to play out scenes. There's no one way or another; it's given so much texture — which I needed. We've got an incredible writer who is always there to help change things if necessary, or to question or to converse with. We speak so much."

Conversations started about the transformation Cooper would undergo weeks before the project started. During production, Cooper has nothing but appreciative words for these "two hilarious guys who are great directors, giving you perfect notes." Heading into the world of *Preacher*, Cooper's opinion of the man he was about to play is a helpful guide:

"Jesse believes that there's something up there, that there's a greater God — that's something that he has to stick to. So, we meet a desperate, lost, self-pitying, dark, damaged human being. He's a man who can see no way out. His life is overshadowed by the guilt of something that he did that he blames himself for, and he genuinely seeks forgiveness."

BELOW: *Jesse contemplates the complexity of life in Annville with a quiet smoke.*

> "Go to Hell, Eugene!"
>
> Jesse

ABOVE: *In a fit of rage Jesse Custer sends a man to Hell. Then drags him back from the depths. But has he...really?*

Showrunner Sam Catlin is the man tasked with containing the wildness that ensues on set, and keeping an overview of what exactly is going on in Annville, Texas, and further beyond.

Catlin's take on the titular hero explores both sides of his personality, which intertwine and sometimes conflict. "When we first meet Jesse he's the quintessential man with a dark and troubled past," Catlin observes. "He's trying to atone for some great sins and transgressions. Part of him is a really good man who wants to be just like his father. But he has another part which is super dark: he loves to drink, he loves to fight, he's the most irreverent preacher in West Texas."

Cooper also points to this battle within Jesse: "He probably thinks he's a bit of a fraud, and a failure. But he's a good man deep down and he's trying his best. Putting his past behind him, making amends

for what he's done." Yet rather than make him weaker, this somehow makes the young preacher an ideal candidate for a power that has torn apart lesser mortals.

Regarding Genesis fulfilling its mystifying purpose through Jesse, Cooper carefully surmises: "I expect it's just that deep down strength that he has, that comes partly from a slight insanity, a refusal to quit or give up. Maybe what it senses is a mind and a spirit that no matter how bad things get it can't quite be destroyed or beaten."

Although, as Catlin suggests, Jesse is "sort of spooked by the fact that he's got this power, because he doesn't trust himself with it", what's more important now is that Jesse has the chance to heal a very deep wound. That wound being the loss of his father, for which he holds himself accountable (and for good reason). Says Cooper,

"Jesse's on a journey of helping this town that his father embraced and held together, which has been crumbling ever since his death. He feels a responsibility towards everyone, and he's confronted by such desperation."

Another perspective on Jesse, offered by Ruth Negga, relates to the core narrative between the two leads. Specifically, time they experienced apart — for reasons initially kept secret — leading to their reunion. Says Negga: "For Jesse, he internalized it and reconsidered his life up to then. There's lots of strands about familial responsibility, passing the baton on, but there's a deep crisis of faith going on with Jesse that is really heavily explored in the pilot."

Meanwhile, there is another, sinister side to Jesse that not even the supposed Will of God can suppress. Jesse may try to forget, but Annville has a way of reminding him that he can really fight. "Not only do we see that Jesse knows how to kick ass," says Catlin, "we also see there's a part of him that loves it. Violence isn't only something he's good at, but he revels in it. This guy, in a way, is the most dangerous man in the world."

BELOW: *The Bible. The Holy Book. But on Preacher if you open the cover you'll see that it's not what it seems.*

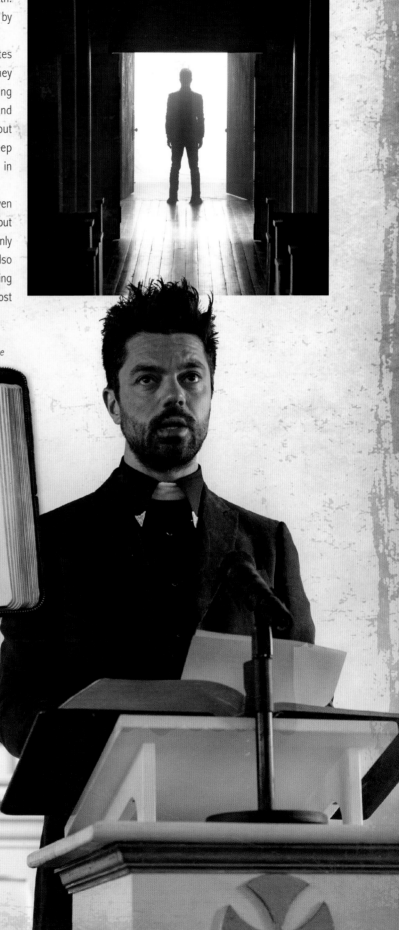

"If God wants our help, we'll help him. If he doesn't, we're gonna kick His ass."

Jesse

ABOVE: *In the beginning Jesse is unsure of his role as a preacher and the choices he made that got him there. But his road is long and much will change on the way.*

Why Jesse is chosen as the vessel for Genesis, we do not know. It is fascinating, however, to witness Jesse as he wrestles with this most peculiar of circumstances, like a ship lost at sea carrying dangerous cargo; some kind of ethereal time bomb. This is not possession, though. Jesse makes up his own mind, with only himself to blame for the harm that befalls people around him. Yet, somehow, even those Jesse hurts the most choose to remain by his side.

Says Ruth Negga, "This Jesse isn't the Jesse that Tulip wanted back. He's not that man any more. She worries that this will be a uniquely corruptible force. You see these flashes in Jesse where there's this thrill, and that disturbs her. She sees that there's a darkness there."

Jesse's initial self-absorbed quest for the spectacular obscures some of the truest needs, which in the case of Tulip is tragic. "He doesn't know the side of her that doesn't have these massive, massive problems. He doesn't know about this side to her life that makes her more fragile. It says quite a lot about Jesse. He had no idea about the past, or her past."

Initially, Genesis is a blessed plaything received as God's gift to a holy man at his wits' end. "He's consumed in the belief that he's become a star in the town," says Cooper of the early events in Annville, which sees parishioner Ted open his heart to his mom, and sworn atheist Odin Quincannon serve God with fatal consequences.

Of the Odin scene, Cooper observes, "While you're watching this unfold, you're discovering that this person is using this in utterly the wrong way. And people are in awe of it. From that moment onwards, he changes dramatically. It's working, but he's enjoying it, and he's getting the wrong type of pleasure with what seems to be quite a spiritual moment."

Ian Colletti, who plays Eugene 'Arseface' Root, offers his perspective on the reasons for being literally damned to Hell in season 1: "I think Eugene works as a mirror for Jesse, in the sense that he reflects back his own vulnerabilities and flaws." For Cooper, it's not the mistake itself that raises his concern: "There's little regret, and that's what's terrifying about Jesse. You can't tell if he really cares at all."

Jesse believing that he is all-powerful carries into season 2, and is devalued by his darker side. Revelations about Tulip's marriage to Victor rouses what Sam Catlin describes as historical anger for keeping secrets. "It's the first time we see Jesse go into this mode where he has this inner death," says Cooper. "It's the worst part of him. You think he's going to absolutely destroy this person [Victor]. Then he goes into this terrifying silence, and that is very frightening."

In spite of everything, Jesse has not lost his mind. It takes a near miss with a demon from Hell to clarify his thoughts, but Jesse realizes that this is not what he wanted. Says Cooper, "Even with his arrogance, or the belief that he should be the person with this power."

TULIP O'HARE

RUTH NEGGA BRINGS arresting depth to *Preacher*'s Priscilla-Jean Henrietta O'Hare, otherwise known as Tulip. When describing her role, it is as though Negga is sculpting Tulip from the inside out, viewing her from every angle. What she does is more than a change of attitude and clothes.

During a career spanning more than a decade, Negga has honed her craft with celebrated performances as Ophelia in *Hamlet* on stage with the UK's National Theatre (2010), and by tackling more fantastical roles such as Lady Taria in *Warcraft*: *The Beginning* (2016). What was it that attracted her to the role of Tulip?

"I had never read such an awesome introduction to a character. Indeed, I hadn't read a female part as unapologetic as

LEFT AND BELOW: Tulip O'Hare: thief, bank robber, improvisational weapon-smith, and best babysitter in the world. A woman of many nefarious talents.

her. It was quite clear Tulip owns the space she takes up; this is no wallflower. Partly because that's her nature, but as a woman of color in a male world she feels determined to be an equal, and that often means making one's presence felt when it is ignored and taken seriously when it is underestimated. The script really captured that for me."

Diving into a role like Tulip O'Hare takes a lot of thought and careful consideration. Negga shares her thoughts on the role she has made her own: "I think Tulip displays a lot of nuance, at least that's what I always try to infuse my characters with. She is extreme only because we are dealing with a comic universe. I just play the human within an extraordinary world."

Sometimes the challenges of playing a deadly assassin are more physical in nature, as Negga divulges with a smile: "With some of those guns I can't even reach the trigger with my tiny fingers!"

With her classical acting background, it isn't so surprising to hear *Preacher* described as "very Greek in nature" by Negga. "It's quite daunting how epic it is," the actress says. "You almost expect a chorus to greet every new scene. Every scene is so well choreographed and put together and written, you worry 'Will I ever do it justice?' I've found that tough. There's so much going on, there's so much that you can do, and so much potential. You can easily become overwhelmed by the epic scale."

Though smart, sensitive and meticulous in her work, Negga readily diverts attention away from herself to the production team and the artistic direction on *Preacher*. "You know, it's always lovely when you read a script that's far cleverer than you are," she says.

"Their output is extraordinary," she says of executives Seth Rogen, Evan Goldberg and Sam Catlin. "I always think, 'Maybe one day I'll write and direct and adapt something'. Then you meet the real deal, and you think, 'No, I'd have to have a lie down. I'd rather lie down.' Their energy is insane — and their attention to detail. Sometimes they'll go for the broad strokes, but then they fine-tune it. Their direction is always super spot-on."

Negga is also swift to highlight the good vibe among cast and crew that was evident from the early stages: "Read-throughs are nerve-wracking. You're wondering if you'll be shown the door as soon as it's over. All the execs were there and it was intimidating," she says. "But everyone was saying, 'Wow, this is super awesome!' when they heard everything coming to life.

"These characters are so big, so fleshy and extreme. Garth Ennis said a brilliant thing: that the characters will be having a chat one minute and then be in a catastrophe the next. We can't help but absorb that. Our energies are kind of developed into a reflection of who we're playing. It's a high-octane piece of work, you know."

"A woman needs to know how to be strong and stand on her own."

Tulip

Monsoon Wedding Chapel

In *Preacher* we learn about Tulip from flashbacks to her difficult childhood, and when she and soulmate Jesse became estranged as adults. Tulip's strong and multi-faceted personality evokes remarkable performances from Negga in every episode.

"*Preacher* is this labyrinthine journey that you're taken on by these three distinct misfits who are sort of the 'every people', actually," says Negga. "Even though they're quite extreme personalities, you can see yourself in a myriad of ways in each of them."

The Tulip encountered in the pilot episode does not immediately show her full colors as a person. Indeed, all the key characters have similar layers of complexity as she does. "They're on a journey questioning their validity as human beings in this world, navigating their relationships with some crazy, crazy stuff," says Negga. "It's very dark — macabre, but funny and pulpy; detailed and…deep. And very, very clever."

When turning to Tulip specifically, Negga highlights a "broken, damaged past" comprising of experiences that the character uses to reconstruct herself, rather than allowing them to fade away.

"There's definitely a vulnerability there, but vulnerability is so complex," says Negga. "She counters this vulnerability with toughness and revenge, by doing something about it. Our Tulip isn't quick to cry, that's just not who she is."

"Tulip, she's a pistol. She's a feisty one, that's what you learn," says producer Sam Catlin. "When we meet her, she feels like a badass beautiful woman with a gun. She is that, but as we get to know her more and more we realize that she also comes from a lot of pain and a lot of heartbreak, and we understand why she acts out."

Although rarely ever being provided with the most conclusive read of Tulip, the audience is often challenged by her apparent extreme, juxtaposed behavior. Reading from the script, Negga was delighted at the prospect of somehow making this seem normal for Tulip.

"I love the scene with the kids at the table, when we're making the homemade bazooka. I loved the scene anyway, before we shot it, because it was like, 'Is she insane?' But the scene is so brilliantly written that you end up going, 'Yeah, this makes sense actually. Of course, they're just having fun and she's the best babysitter in the world!' If the bazooka wasn't there, it would be really cool arts and crafts. Let's make something cool, let's have some fun. And then… it's a bazooka."

Again, Negga nods respectfully toward the producers and the kinds of risks they are willing to take to retain the show's bizarre authenticity. "That's the thing about Tulip. You're going, 'Um, morally, the bazooka…?' But she doesn't care," asserts Negga. "She cares about the kids' safety, but she's got a job to do. The great thing about Tulip is that Sam, Evan and Seth aren't afraid to bypass 'we have to justify this.' She's not maternal, but she's good fun!"

ABOVE: *Tulip asks what Genesis really is. This is how Jesse shows her. Tulips follows up with a punch to his face and instructions never to do it again.*

1972 CHEVROLET CHEVELLE SS

While Tulip is mending a broken "art thing" for one her kids, Emily Woodrow interrupts the awkward silence by commenting on the amazing vehicle parked outside. "That's a nice car," says Emily. To which Tulip recites: "'72 Chevelle SS. Crate 350 with a cowl induction hood and 4.11 gears. Flowmaster. T/A Tires." Information which may fly over the heads of most people.

Breaking this down, the SS stands for Super Sport, which refers to the name of the package. Crate 350 is the engine, a high-performance replacement part; a motor shipped in a crate. The number describes an internal displacement of 350 cubic inches. The cowl is an option that provided forced air induction to cool the engine. 4.11 gears are the final drive ratio that sacrifices economy for ridiculous acceleration. Flowmaster is the muffler. T/A tires are the muscle-car radials of choice, and the T/A stands for the Trans Am racing series in the US.

As Emily says: a nice car.

God, I love my car!

Central to *Preacher*'s main story arc is the relationship between Jesse Custer and Tulip, described succinctly by Ruth Negga as "ex-lovers and partners-in-crime." Although a third, significant character enters the frame in the form of a vampire called Cassidy, it's the core duo, and their motto Until the End of the World, that captivates us with their affairs.

"It's not blatantly clear, their shenanigans, but you get the idea that Tulip and Jesse were involved in some shady business," says Negga. "Something happened that created a chasm between them, and they went their separate ways. There's a very present tension. They're both circling each other, very wary of each other, and it's very obvious that hearts were hurt, and something serious happened that brought their relationship to an end."

Dominic Cooper says of Jesse and Tulip that, "They are each other's absolute soulmates. They can't really function or live without one another. Or absolutely with each other, either. Their relationship is the catalyst for everything."

Even while Tulip and Jesse are apart, they consider themselves to be together in some way, although as events unfold Tulip appears to be more conscious of this. Says Negga, "You get the sense that Tulip went off and carried on doing what she was really good at. Jesse's journey has been very different. They have both been dealing with whatever trauma happened to them in different ways."

When we first see Tulip and Jesse reunited, the roles seem clear. Tulip needs her man back to continue with their adventures and rekindle the love affair. "It's too easy," says Negga. "She sees it as too easy. When you've been best buddies with someone for so long, and you grow up and you've still got that energy, and they're like 'I just want to take it easy for a bit' but you're like, 'No way, man! We had something amazing, why are you ruining it?'"

Even here, though, we don't need to scratch too deep beneath the surface to see something else behind Tulip's determined gaze. "I think there's a deep hurt, and also an anger. Maybe there's retribution to be had…" Eventually we do learn all there is to know, and it is tough.

Occasionally with Tulip — via Negga's performance — it is her response to the actions of those around her that reveals the most about her. She is the one who demonstrates the greatest dissonance with Jesse's newfound mission, that something isn't right with it. When Jesse tells Tulip that she can be good, she can't get her head around it.

"That he can go from being, essentially, the other half of her, to being this changed, saved soul is a deep shock to her," Negga says. "It's like a little dart to her heart. And he knows it. I think that she's winded by him saying that, because it's deeply personal."

BELOW: *Our intro to Tulip involves a knife and gun fight, a speeding car in a corn field, ear-biting, and a "very bad man". Things then move on to arts and crafts.*

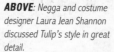

ABOVE: *Negga and costume designer Laura Jean Shannon discussed Tulip's style in great detail.*

TULIP'S STYLE

Tulip's appearance speaks volumes about the spirit residing within. Costume designer Laura Jean Shannon worked closely with Ruth Negga to achieve the precise look that the actress believed to be correct.

"What I didn't want to be was a clothes horse," Negga states. "I was thinking of women I admire, who are very creative in the way they dress, but who have an authenticity about it. It's not lifted straight from a magazine. They kind of dress by osmosis. It's like how they are inside, a deep reflection of their art and who they are. People came to mind like FKA Twigs, M.I.A., and Bat for Lashes. Tulip is not just this gun for hire, you know, who doesn't give a toss what she looks like. You can be this awesome, hard, kick-ass queen and still really care about artistic expression and the way you look."

Negga and 'L.J.' met before production on the show started to figure out how Tulip's soul could take shape from the inside and out. "You need both," says Negga. "I don't have one way of working, and sometimes you find that a look just changes the way you see someone; it creates an access point. Sometimes the clothes provide a cover."

There was also the creative direction of the show to consider, to stay in line with the aesthetic that producers Seth, Evan and Sam wanted. "The guys mentioned Rhianna," states Negga. "I was thinking of the comic, sort of like early 1990s cut-offs, t-shirts, a *Thelma & Louise* kind of thing. I think they wanted to bring it into the modern day. There are 90s influences, little touches here and there, but they wanted to make it pop now, and not be a period piece."

L.J. and Negga very soon found themselves working on the same wavelength, with the costume designer encouraging contributions for ideas that the actress found refreshing. Things turned out well for them both. "We wanted Tulip to feel sexy, because Tulip does feel sexy. She's the complete opposite of a shrinking violet or a wallflower — everything about her body, she owns. Many women who are physically tough and able, the way they hold themselves is very outstanding and attractive. They feel sexy, whatever that means to them."

The resulting, carefully selected wardrobe aided the actress' performance. Recalls Negga: "We chose things that made me feel that way, as Tulip. It doesn't need to be about flesh, it can be about popping colors or putting strange things together. She has body confidence, and what L.J. put together helped me a lot."

"We are who we are, and that's it, you know? Why waste another minute wishin' we were different?"

Tulip

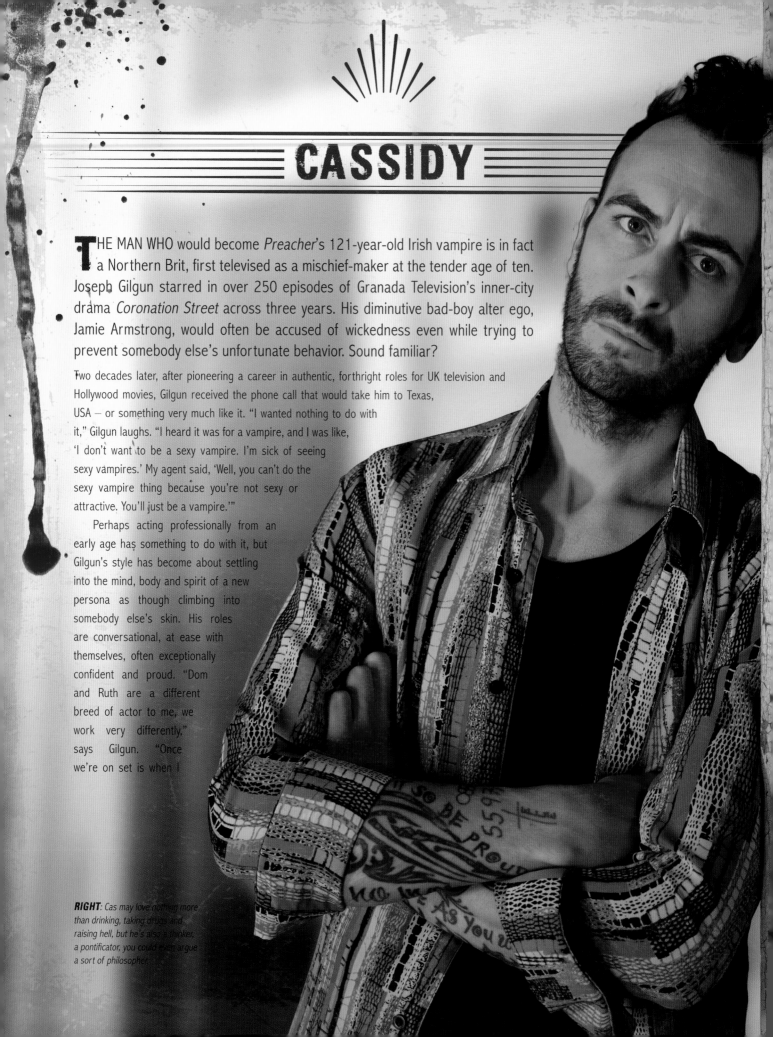

CASSIDY

THE MAN WHO would become *Preacher*'s 121-year-old Irish vampire is in fact a Northern Brit, first televised as a mischief-maker at the tender age of ten. Joseph Gilgun starred in over 250 episodes of Granada Television's inner-city drama *Coronation Street* across three years. His diminutive bad-boy alter ego, Jamie Armstrong, would often be accused of wickedness even while trying to prevent somebody else's unfortunate behavior. Sound familiar?

Two decades later, after pioneering a career in authentic, forthright roles for UK television and Hollywood movies, Gilgun received the phone call that would take him to Texas, USA — or something very much like it. "I wanted nothing to do with it," Gilgun laughs. "I heard it was for a vampire, and I was like, 'I don't want to be a sexy vampire. I'm sick of seeing sexy vampires.' My agent said, 'Well, you can't do the sexy vampire thing because you're not sexy or attractive. You'll just be a vampire.'"

Perhaps acting professionally from an early age has something to do with it, but Gilgun's style has become about settling into the mind, body and spirit of a new persona as though climbing into somebody else's skin. His roles are conversational, at ease with themselves, often exceptionally confident and proud. "Dom and Ruth are a different breed of actor to me, we work very differently," says Gilgun. "Once we're on set is when I

RIGHT: *Cas may love nothing more than drinking, taking drugs and raising hell, but he's also a thinker, a pontificator, you could even argue a sort of philosopher.*

can start figuring stuff out. We talk a lot about our work on set and the intention of where we're going with the scene, where we're going with the characters. I don't have to tell them [what I've changed], I'll just do it and they feel it, we work around one another."

Credit is also due to casting director Linda Lowy, and Sam Catlin who insisted that Seth Rogen check out this guy. "I did a call with Sam, Seth and Evan. I was in my bedroom, living with one of my best friends," recalls Gilgun. "I just remember talking to these lads, and thinking, 'They're all really good human beings.' I remember looking at Seth — and he's so kind, such a lovely guy — thinking, 'I'll easily survive this. As long as they're there, I'll survive this.'"

An unusual choice of words, 'survive', until you learn that Joe has bipolar disorder. "At the time I was going through a serious bout of depression, which was married with a bad bout of anxiety," Gilgun explains. "They call it GAD — general anxiety disorder — and that was a brand new feeling for me. So, there was this big risk there for me."

Gilgun has since been praised for being pitch-perfect as Cassidy, fully embodying the wild role. Clearly, Gilgun is enjoying the experience so far. "I've been very fortunate to be working alongside people like Sam, Seth, Evan, Ruth and Dom. I'm working with a group of people who are constantly trying to get the best out of themselves, and out of one another. None of us ever walk away, going, 'nailed.' That's just the job. That's the nature of what we do."

ABOVE: An off-duty moment. What's tickled Ruth, we wonder?
LEFT: Joseph Gilgun — an actor with highly expressive eyebrows.

VAMPIRE INK

The tattoos on Cassidy's body are real, and very personal to the actor Joseph Gilgun who has been featured as one of the most heavily tattooed men in Hollywood. His body art is so prominent that it has been worked into the script, with Jesse commenting in season 1, episode 6 'Sundowner', "You look like a men's room wall." To which Cassidy admits, "I went through a period of low impulse control."

It is reported that Gilgun has the names of two co-stars over his butt, in addition to the word LOL on his right hand, referring to his fictional sweetheart Frances Lorraine 'Lollipop Lol' Jenkins in TV series *This is England*. His left sleeve carries the phrase "make the most of it", alongside "Mum" and "Dad." There was a danger that continuity would be ruined after Gilgun inked another tattoo on his chest between *Preacher* seasons. As a consequence, Gilgun was asked to shave his chest so that concealer could be applied.

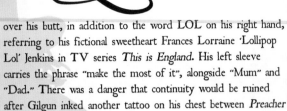

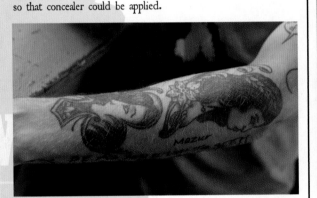

Cassidy's bombastic antics tend to involve Gilgun in the more chaotic side of the shooting schedule, and the actor has nothing but praise for those behind the scenes. "They never get a day off from start to finish. Those men and women are unbelievable. They've got endless, boundless energy that if you could bottle it you'd make a bloody fortune."

As the show has progressed, Gilgun says that the producers turned up the heat. "Seth, Sam and Evan wanted to bring a bit of reality to that whole journey. Which could be stressful at times," says Gilgun. "Come the second season when I had to dig deep with Denis, it became a challenge then. Whatever my character goes through, I seem to wind up going through eventually." This moves our discussion onto something especially important about Cassidy that the actor needs you to know:

"When I did my first year, I did Comicon. There was a question about how different I am to Cassidy, and I made this huge joke, and said 'I don't have to dig deep, I'm a drug-addict lunatic.' And that's not true." Gilgun discloses. "I said that because I wanted to entertain 6,000 people stood in front of me. I wanted to make them laugh. The reality is we're very different, me and Cassidy. Very different. For a lot of the audience, they don't see that.

"A lot of people that meet me in the street, members of the public, fans of the show, often assume that I'm going to be Cassidy, and the person they're meeting is Cass. The number of times people have said, 'You're just like him. It's brilliant to meet you, you're just the same as you are on the TV.' But I'm not.

"There are moments where I have to dig very deep, and it can be quite damaging. That's what I want the public to know. It's not always a walk in the park being Cassidy. I do have to find him. It's important for the fans of the show to know that it's not always easy. It's not. When you have to cry, and you have to dig deep, it hurts.

"Me and Cassidy are two completely different human beings."

Gilgun compares his methodology, and the culmination of each project, to running at full speed into a brick wall. "You run and run because you're scared someone will catch you. Suddenly it stops, everybody goes home, and you go straight into this brick wall.

"I talked to a therapist about this not long ago. I felt corny, like one of these actors that says 'I embody my character,' and all that bullshit. But you actually do," imparts Gilgun. "If you're pretending to be a guy, every day, five days of the week, it's inevitable that you're going to change a little bit. Being that you've embodied this made-up character, and you've slowly become him, when you go back home, you have to go back to being you again. That transition is very difficult for me."

ABOVE AND ABOVE RIGHT: As a vampire who often skates way over the line into lawlessness, it's inevitable that Cass sometimes ends up inside a jail cell.

Creator and writer of the original comic book series, Garth Ennis, says how "Cassidy is the wild card in all of this. He crashes into the middle of the story, and nothing's the same afterwards – which is very Cassidy." Ennis' snapshot of the role as "an Irish vampire who's been living in the States for over 100 years and is loving every minute of it" has been hungrily adopted by Gilgun who, unsurprisingly, has a little more to say on the matter.

"One of the things that was so inviting about the role was that this guy was just constantly having a good time: misbehaving, fighting on planes, doing drugs. He was just good fun. It saved me, you know," confides Gilgun. "By becoming this guy, on and off set, it pulled me out of this gloom, because I had to be someone else. Eventually it started to eat into my personal life. I started to have much more fun."

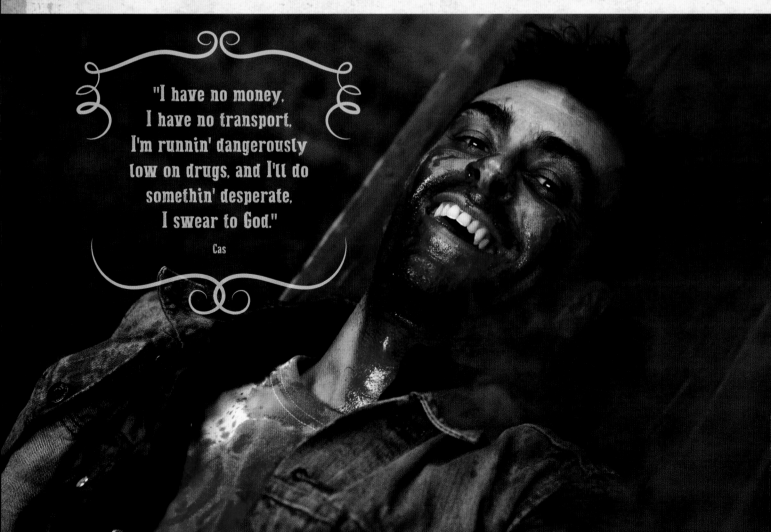

"I have no money,
I have no transport,
I'm runnin' dangerously
low on drugs, and I'll do
somethin' desperate,
I swear to God."

Cas

If you know the actor, however, the performance delves much deeper to where an element of pathos is impossible to overlook and bravely embraced. Gilgun's portrayal of Woody in *This is England* demonstrated how tenderly a joker can behave toward his truest friends. And this also impacted the storyline involving Denis, and Cassidy's estranged family.

"Initially, I think it was meant to be a bit of a gag, that Cassidy had an eighty-year-old son. The gag was the juxtaposition between how Cassidy looks, and this old man. He spoke French, and Cassidy didn't speak any French. Denis doesn't know any English and there's this whole language barrier. But they ended up developing him into this really beautiful storyline."

There is another side to all this, however, as Gilgun goes on to explain. "Cassidy is dark, man. He's been a bad guy. For those fans that are watching the show that haven't read the comic, Cassidy's a bad person, he's done some terrible things. He's not just good fun, he's also a complete bastard. If you cross him, if you make a mistake, he'll just leave you, just like he did his son. He abandoned Denis for eighty years. And when he did see him, it would be on Cassidy's terms, generally because of drugs. Imagine smoking crack cocaine, and injecting heroin with prostitutes in your child's house. The reality of that is fucked up."

"Cassidy is a light-hearted guy. He's sort of the comedy element within the storyline of the pilot, but Cassidy has really serious problems. He's 121 years old, and he's miserable. He wants to feel the sun," Gilgun adds. "What's interesting about *Preacher*, what they've done with Cassidy, is that you don't usually see this side of vampires. Since meeting Jesse and Tulip, there's a lot of inner turmoil because he doesn't want to leave. But then, if he stays, they'll only die eventually. He's jostling with a lot of internal trauma."

Producer Evan Goldberg shares his view on tragic Cass: "I think Cassidy is a tragic hero. He is a very honorable guy at times, but he has this innate nature where he's self-destructive, and he's going to do something bad to himself and everyone around him, eventually."

THAT SUNBURN

Toward the close of the pilot episode, Jesse Custer renews his vows to the church, making a series of promises to his congregation. It is a very powerful moment, and we would like to believe him. As part of his mission, Jesse pledges to "welcome those who are lost", at which point our attention is drawn to Cassidy, enjoying a beer in the shade and holding his arm in sunlight, thus allowing his left hand to catch fire. It's a superb special effect, with the realism due to the flames being real.

How did they make it look so convincing, without scarring Gilgun for the rest of his life?

"They cover your skin in fire-proof gel, and they have a wire that runs up here [shirt sleeve] which is essentially an electric match," Gilgun confides. "The 'match' ignites this flammable liquid, literally designed for setting people on fire. I'm trying to sound like I know what I'm talking about. I haven't a clue. It didn't burn me."

Gilgun depicts Cassidy's world-weariness with aplomb, brilliantly observed as a character the actor describes with a glass half empty, whereas for Jesse there is still hope. "Cassidy is a lifelong sceptic," says Gilgun. "He's seen that Jesse wants to be a new human being. Initially, I think Cassidy finds that farcical and dishonest. 'Keep it real, be who you are,' which is a killer. Jesse obviously doesn't listen to Cass — he's on a much higher path."

"Cassidy can't believe Jesse is at one with the Lord," Cooper points out. "And he's right."

The bond between Cassidy and Jesse is swift to take after a chance encounter ahead of a bar room brawl. Jesse trusts Cassidy with his secret, which makes perfect sense to Gilgun. "Cassidy is somebody you can go to. He's not going to judge you, because he's nuts — who is he to judge?" The scene from season 1, in which the friends take Jesse's power for a ride, contrasts with a much bleaker relationship in later episodes, when the opposite seems true.

Cassidy falls in love with Tulip, against his better judgement. It's a truth that he cannot allow to fade, no matter what the consequences. "I think with Tulip, he adores her, and he's not for giving up," Gilgun explains. "He's too long in the tooth to be hanging on for people's feelings. He wants to know, get to the bottom of it, 'Let's not waste any time.'" They don't, which adds to the complications further down the line, when Cassidy needs to pick a side.

Ruth Negga shares her view of such an ill-fated relationship: "Cassidy does understand Tulip's need for vengeance, and bloodthirst. I think because Cassidy has been hunted all his life,

and they have a deep need to settle scores."

"With Tulip and Cass, it's the honor amongst thieves," Gilgun elaborates, on the occasion involving Tulip's apparent abduction. "It is a massive deceit, and he's right in the middle of it all. It's a nightmare. He's not prepared to let her die. His intention is to go in that house and do the right thing by his friend, do the right thing by the two of them as a couple.

"I don't think Cassidy questions it for one second. He'll do whatever it takes. He does adore Tulip, and that shows us a side to Cassidy. That's the side you trust, that you can rely on."

Speaking of those close to him, the conversation lightens up when referring to Gilgun's real life family, and how he'd explain Cassidy and *Preacher* to them. "If you were one of me fam, and you were asking what am I doing at the moment, I'd say 'I'm playing an Irish vampire, and he's dead sexy.' And they'd go, 'Oooh, what's it like?' and I'd say, 'Well, he's a drug addict.' And it always gets a brilliant reaction."

"I can't describe the show, I've tried a million times," laughs Gilgun. "It's a bit like *Punisher*, but it's nothing like *Punisher*. It's a bit like *Interview with the Vampire*, meets *Fear and Loathing in Las Vegas*, they have a sex orgy and produce this bastard child."

Finally, amusing but also very true, Gilgun has been especially diligent when it comes to respecting Cassidy's heritage. "The main people I want to convince are the Irish, I don't want to do a bad accent," says Gilgun. "I don't want Irish people watching me going, 'Jesus Christ, he's just ruining our native tongue!' Working alongside Ruth, if there's anything I'm unsure about I'll ask her. She's very complimentary."

FLIGHT & FIGHT

A special set was built to contain Cassidy's wild introduction in the pilot episode of *Preacher*. We lead in gently, with mischievous talk of *hamster del culo* and such from Cass to his supposed hedge-fund buddies. This is before Cass heads to the restroom where he learns the truth from a heavily (and strangely) annotated Bible: the men he's trapped with on the plane know his secret and are out to slay him — although they are certainly *not* fully prepared for a Cass fight.

The sequence is a minute long, swiftly cutting between Joseph Gilgun and his stunt double Solomon Brende, who sums up the

> "How did you wankers find me then?"
>
> Cassidy

ABOVE: *Ever the opportunist, Cassidy fights with whatever tools come to hand, the more combustible the better.*

ABOVE: *This is the smartest dressed we see Cassidy. After this scene it's strictly casual - although the bloodstains reappear frequently.*

combat as "a one-on-five fight, including a fire burn, with a bunch of medieval weapons." The scenario rapidly shifts to a larger-than-life ruckus in which battle axes, crossbows and spears unexpectedly appear, in between Cassidy hurling silver service trays and igniting an aerosol into a fiery blaze. It ends with Cass decanting a bottle of blood from the dying plane captain to use to recuperate after his next trick: freefalling to the ground with only an umbrella to slow his descent.

As Evan Goldberg exclaims: "The fights are rad. Come on, dude!"

Although we do see a gentleman who looks very much like Gilgun tumbling toward Texas, we should confirm that this wasn't the man himself. "No, I won't be jumping out of a plane on the day; that's a terrifying idea," verifies Gilgun before the shoot. "We have somebody else to do that."

Incredibly, this isn't the craziest of shenanigans that our new favorite vampire excels in as the show gathers momentum. There are far more serious opponents in the weeks to come.

RIGHT: *Even in the midst of a fight Cass is sharp enough to try to get some information.*

ALL SAINTS CHURCH

PREACHER

ALL SAINTS CHURCH
INTERIOR STAGE SET

KITCHEN

STORAGE CLOSET

COMMON ROOM

BACK DOOR

ACCORDION DOOR

TO COMMON ROOM

STAIRS TO ATTIC

2ND DOOR TO ATTIC STAIRS

BATHROOM

FAMILY LIVING ROOM

ALTAR

EXIT

BALCONY

FOYER

FRONT DOOR

POCKET DOOR

JESSE'S BEDROOM

YOUNG JESSE BEDROOM

You are invited to take a tour of All Saint's Congregational Church in 360-degree VR via the AMC website and Google Cardboard, or through your browser on a conventional screen. In either case, you can appreciate the faithfulness with which the Custers' family chapel was constructed for the show. It needed to be, since All Saints features in eight of nine episodes from season 1 plus the pilot, with only 'Finish the Song' focused solely on events elsewhere.

In the pilot, we see Jesse deliver a bleary-eyed sermon to a pitiful throng, with even those in attendance being distracted somehow. At this point All Saints' has no discernable sense of the spiritual; it's just a room lined with creaking benches that swallows the efforts of Emily Woodrow's music-making on the organ, which simply sounds out of date. It's so awkward.

The church later becomes the scene of Jesse's encounter with the comet, and subsequent possession by Genesis, which leaves him unconscious for three days. From Jesse's desperate prayers that

GLENN FABRY

1861 - 1932

ONCE UPON A TIME

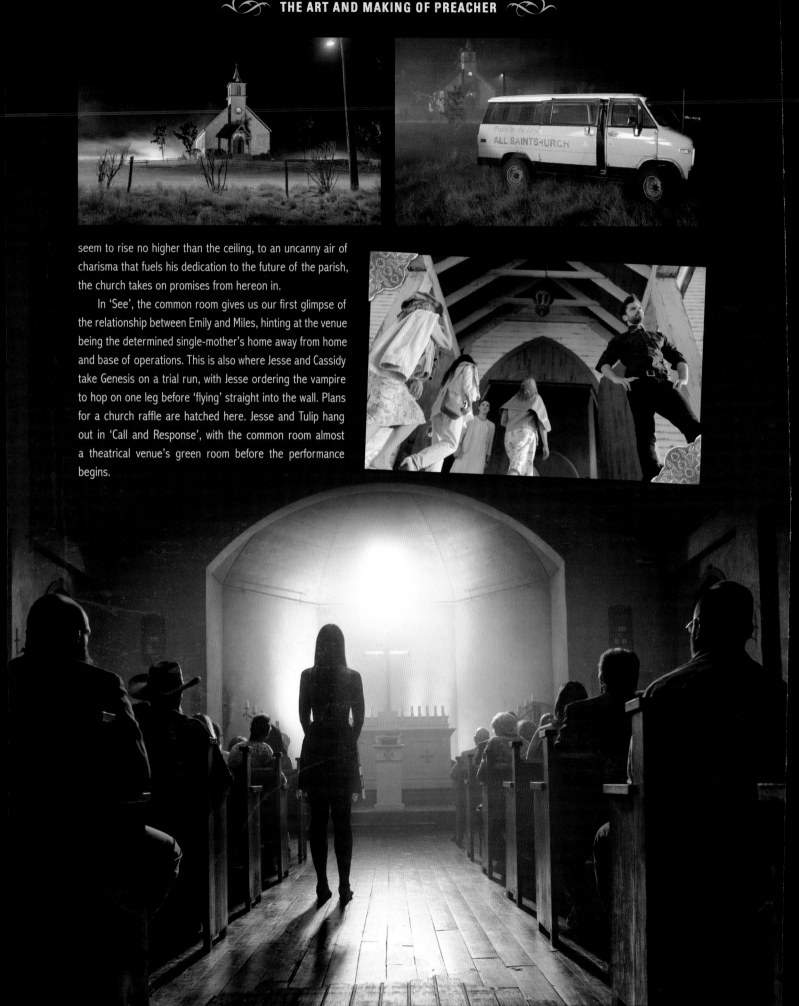

seem to rise no higher than the ceiling, to an uncanny air of charisma that fuels his dedication to the future of the parish, the church takes on promises from hereon in.

In 'See', the common room gives us our first glimpse of the relationship between Emily and Miles, hinting at the venue being the determined single-mother's home away from home and base of operations. This is also where Jesse and Cassidy take Genesis on a trial run, with Jesse ordering the vampire to hop on one leg before 'flying' straight into the wall. Plans for a church raffle are hatched here. Jesse and Tulip hang out in 'Call and Response', with the common room almost a theatrical venue's green room before the performance begins.

When we journey to the past, we see young Jesse praying in his bedroom, which is also on site. Details lost in the shadows of this pivotal scene include an Etch-A-Sketch propped up against the wall, a shelf cluttered with tiny robots and model cars, and a Wild West mural that mightv have inspired Jesse's dreams before they became nightmares.

The exterior becomes symbolic too, as a focal point for Odin Quincannon's ruthless greed. This allows for the hilarious standoff between Jesse and Quincannon's 'meat men', which results in the loss of something very precious, and shows Jesse's darker side and cruel sense of mirth. At the close of season 1, the first we know of Annville's destruction is a flash of white light that plays across the walls before the building is swept away in the blast. With All Saints wiped out, we know that there is no turning back as Jesse and his friends hit the road.

ABOVE AND BELOW: *As with all the sets for the show each room on All Saints is constructed and lit with an intense eye for character and detail.*

EUGENE 'ARSEFACE' ROOT

IAN COLLETTI'S STRENGTH as an actor allows him to portray the character of Eugene Root as a mirror reflecting all manner of immoral and despicable activity. We cling to Colletti's wonderful portrayal of innocence, absolving him of wrongdoing when somebody else is to blame.

Whether this is the character of Myles Holt in Ted Geoghegan's *Mohawk* (2017), where he joins his father on a reprehensible murderous quest, or the son of hapless criminal defense lawyer in *Rake* (2014), through Colletti we eventually question everything. It enables *Preacher*'s infamous Arseface to become a character we care a great deal about, perhaps more than we expect.

"The first thing that attracted me to playing Eugene was the world that he inhabits," Colletti says. "Through the audition process, I took a crash course in all-things *Preacher* and I was blown away by the horrifying (and hysterical) universe that Garth Ennis and Steve Dillon had created. It's an actor's playground; I was thrilled by the idea of getting to live in it as Eugene.

"Whether he's acting as Jesse's conscience in season 1, or going through his own personal journey in season 2, his role is to bring up important topics like suffering, forgiveness and redemption. I really believe he is the moral center of *Preacher*."

When Seth Rogen was asked who he was most excited to see being brought to life, he called out Arseface/Eugene first of all. Sam Catlin sums up the role of Eugene in the show as "the truest Christian, the purest of heart, and the most humble and religious," and who's unafraid to confront Jesse Custer on God-fearing matters.

With Eugene comes a host of complex relationships newly formed or in retrospect explored, presenting Colletti with much to consider

going into the role.

"We are very fortunate to have Sam Catlin as our showrunner, backed by a dedicated team of writers, all of whom are willing to answer any of our questions," says Colletti. "It's a learning process. With every script I read, I understand a little bit more. In some instances, it wasn't until after I watched the season air that I went 'Ah, I get it.' I think part of that is because, when you're in the thick of shooting, you're looking at the story through the lens of the character you're playing. But watching it back, you kind of get a birds-eye view on the story, and you can watch the pieces of these relationships fall together."

ABOVE AND RIGHT: *We feel for Eugene for everything he endures. His mutilated mouth means his eyes carry more weight of expression — sadness, desperation, a yearning to be loved.*

'Arseface' cannot hide what happened to him by closing the door on his private life in the same way that Donnie Schenck does. Eugene's tragedy is personal, but as Sam Catlin says of the character, "Because he's such a nice kid, he feels guilty about the burden that his own past has put on his father." Think of the sadness in Eugene's eyes when confronting Hugo Root's outrage. Eugene also, in Catlin's words, "has a terrible knack for putting into words the exact dark thing that's going on with Jesse." And this, of course, is what gets him banished to Hell.

RIGHT AND FAR RIGHT: *Eugene in happier, less mutilated times, and the events that led to the disaster.*

As we later discover in detail, Eugene's own personal Hell is the suicide of Tracy Loach, for which he still blames himself. But when Jesse uses his power to compel forgiveness from Tracy's distraught mother Terri, we see how Eugene is uncomfortable with this.

"For Jesse it's less about Eugene and more about having the town see how powerful this is," Colletti observes. "There's a moment of relief and amazement, and although there's no denying it's a miracle I'm not sure Eugene is convinced it was *God's* miracle. Eugene feels very strongly that people have free will. People have the ability to choose."

In Hell, Eugene's moral compass is severely tested when he meets Adolf Hitler. It seems that Eugene can abide reliving his worst memory over and over again; the real conflict now is between wanting to escape the worst possible prison imaginable and putting his trust in the worst possible soul ever to have stalked the earth.

Says Catlin, "Hitler, oddly, shows some kindness to Eugene. Kindness is a scarce commodity in Hell, and that conflicts with everything he knows. This is Hell, and people are evil, and they're hostile to Hitler, because he's so weak now and he's not intimidating. He makes Eugene start to question his whole belief system.

"Really, of everyone that should not be in Hell, it's Eugene. Hitler recognizes that. Depending on your interpretation, he either takes Eugene under his wing or he takes advantage of Eugene's innocence."

To escape from Hell, Eugene first needs to escape from himself. "Eugene does feel like he belongs in Hell," says Colletti. "All the people around him are telling him this is what he deserves." Meanwhile, Hitler seems genuinely concerned and willing to help, proving that he knows a way out. Eugene is allowed to observe Hitler's worst memory, which is pathetic in almost every sense of the word. As Colletti puts it, "Eugene feels about Hitler's memory the same way I think the audience will feel. Like, 'Really?'"

Observes Colletti, "What makes this show different than any previous project I've been a part of is its unique tone. In the second season, my character is literally in Hell and watches the love of his life blow her head off with a shotgun because he kissed her. But, somehow, it's kinda funny! That is a really crazy balance to find. And it's one that everyone on the show has to find at some point. *Preacher* is filled with absolutely awful things happening all the time, but we often end up finding humor in these moments. It's a lot of fun!"

Ultimately, Eugene finds himself on another guilt-ridden road to redemption after watching Hitler make a break for freedom immediately upon their return to our world.

Oh, Eugene.

ABOVE: *Despite everything — like having an arse face — Eugene puts on a brave front.*

"I don't think God wants me to be there. He's mad at me."

Eugene Root

SHERIFF HUGO ROOT

W. EARL BROWN is an actor with an ability to convince an audience that the characters he plays have not only led a life, but also lived every moment of it. His perceptive portrayals show characters developing a sense of justice, and then doing what's right by regular folk.

In *Preacher*, Brown gives Sheriff Hugo Root a sense of humanity that we can associate with. His job as sheriff ensures that he has built up a litany of examples of why "this world" can be such a terrible, terrible place. Therefore, who can blame him for always being on his guard?

In season 1, episode 3 'The Possibilities', Hugo cautions angels DeBlanc and Fiore with details of a police case involving a family visiting an

ABOVE: As Annville's Sheriff, Hugo Root has to deal with a lot of strange occurrences.

ABOVE: It might take his son going missing to remind him, but Hugo loves Eugene.

amusement park. It is not a happy tale, but the twists and turns that lead us through fear, hope, happiness then despair are formed and told so succinctly by Hugo it clearly shows how this story has played over and over inside his mind.

Painfully aware of the hurt inside his community, and with his own son at the epicenter of the most appalling upset in living memory, Hugo Root is a pressure cooker ready to explode.

On the scene at the kitchen table where Hugo blasts his loving son Eugene, Brown is so convincing that we almost involuntarily turn away and miss whatever is up next. But this parental incident involves a great deal more than spoiled breakfast, and Brown's view is worth hearing.

"I don't think he hates his son. I think that Eugene, having been a part of whatever people think happened, has cast such aspersions at his family, and Hugo blames that on Eugene. And it comes out, in that moment of vile ugliness."

"It's a monster swamp.
Murder. Mayhem.
Escaped lunatics.
Goddam monster swamp."

Sheriff Root

ABOVE AND BELOW: *Over the course of the story Sheriff Root's already jaded view of the world is thrown into even weirder relief.*

THE FATHER, THE SON

Although unable to suppress the anger he feels toward his self-mutilated offspring, Sheriff Hugo Root (W. Earl Brown) cannot in good conscience ignore his paternal bond with hapless Eugene (Ian Colletti). The impression we are given of Sheriff Root is a man who strives to be better because he has seen the very worst. He trusts nobody – and this includes Jesse Custer because of his dark past – but loves his son despite everything that has happened.

Eugene wishes only to please – a near impossible task where his father is concerned, owing to the disgrace that he's brought upon the entire family. Eugene knows of, and tearfully accepts, his father's wrath towards him. It takes Eugene's disappearance for the Sheriff to become actively concerned, while Eugene dwells upon his own worth in Hell.

ABOVE AND RIGHT: *As god-fearin' folk and regular church-goers, what did the Roots do to deserve so much bad luck?*

DEBLANC & FIORE

IF YOU THOUGHT the pilot episode was challenging viewing, episode 1 'See' confirms just how much of a brutal and bizarre rollercoaster ride *Preacher* is. Anatol Yusef and Tom Brooke, in their respective roles as angels DeBlanc and Fiore, bring a chainsaw and a tin coffee can to extract a divine *something* from Jesse as he lies unconscious on the floor of his own church.

"I think the script calls it 'a chainsaw caesarean'," Brooke explains about the grisly operation. "I don't think there would be anyone else as bad at what they're trying to do. It's really embarrassing. We each have our own approach: DeBlanc thinks it's a good idea to sing to it, because it has enjoyed that in the past." 'It' being Genesis, currently understood by Jesse Custer to be the Word of God.

Joseph Gilgun (Cassidy) completes the angels' profile, with some amusement: "They don't know why Jesse's got it. They don't know why it's escaped. All they know is that it's their job to bring it back. And because they're not used to life on Earth, they're pretty bloody useless at it."

BELOW: *DeBlanc and Fiore are on a serious mission, and are seriously out of their depth.*

ABOVE: *Adrift in a strange world with only his friend DeBlanc, Fiore often looks anxious and furtive. Little does he know the trauma that lies in wait.*

When we first see DeBlanc and Fiore, they look like the men for the job — whatever that job may be. They are purposeful, striding with confidence and in possession of all the necessary equipment.

"DeBlanc and Fiore, they've been given a job to be custodians of a power. A power that resides in another world, and is now inside Jesse," informs Yusef. The chainsaw battle that ensues upon the angels' initial encounter with Jesse and guardian Cassidy is plainly disastrous. Even with DeBlanc and Fiore's power to instantaneously resurrect upon death does not give them the edge over a vampire looking out for his mate.

"It's probably the first time they've experienced too much pain," says Sam Catlin.

"It's a messy old fight. They're not fighters, and they're going up against somebody who does it on a daily basis, *and* who's already drunk," adds Brooke, whose character Fiore loses an arm in the struggle.

"It's the first time we realize that DeBlanc and Fiore might not be as dangerous and mysterious as we thought they were," summarizes Yusef. "They might be a couple of incompetent fools, literally not knowing what on Earth they're doing."

Cassidy, of course, is swift to pounce on the vulnerability of these incompetent emissaries, wanting to get to the bottom of this compelling new mystery that is surprising even to him. Catlin explains Cassidy's thoughts: "DeBlanc and Fiore are not vampire vigilantes. Now he realizes that what they want is Jesse's power. They don't seem like they have all the answers."

"I think he's slowly figuring out that we might be idiots, because we give him anything he needs." Yusef says, before offering insight into DeBlanc's train of thought. "I think DeBlanc supposes that however it plays out, they're getting closer to Jesse. Closer to the power."

Brooke has fond memories of preparing for the role of Fiore: "I remember the audition scene was really funny: Fiore is masturbating in a hotel bathroom but not understanding why he's doing it, and DeBlanc is explaining it to him through the door! After that I read the comics and did ask a few questions, but Seth, Evan and Sam just said, 'Don't worry about it, we're not doing the books. All you need to know is our angels are from London.' That was fine. The writing on *Preacher* is first class so what your character says and does usually answers any questions. So something would happen in an episode and you go, 'Oh, so he's *that* kind of guy'."

Rather than the show developing into Angels versus Preacher, the group attempts a more civilized approach to negotiations. DeBlanc and Fiore explain why Jesse ought to return custody of Genesis to them, whereupon Jesse uses the power to bounce the truth out of DeBlanc.

"I think the beginning of episode 6 encapsulates the world of *Preacher* brilliantly," says Yusef. "When Jesse uses the Word of God on DeBlanc and Fiore, it's the first true confirmation that he has our 'baby'." As we later realize, Genesis is a demonic duck call. According to DeBlanc, "Genesis isn't a power, it's a scandal" before being, um, interrupted.

"I think they were expecting Jesse to say, 'Oh well, listen, if that's the case then here you go, have it back'," says Brooke. But, as Yusef confirms, "He's not going to give it back."

Sam Catlin: "DeBlanc and Fiore show up, trying to tell him that the power that he has has nothing to do with God. Jesse thought that he was chosen to have this power. He's all of a sudden gotten this crash course on heavenly politics. He's just reeling, trying to take in all this new information."

Although Jesse bargains with the angels to release Eugene from Hell and allows Genesis to be extracted in return, the entity escapes its tin can cage to resume residence in the preacher.

"I think they've kind of realized they can't do it. They've failed their mission," says Yusef. "The option they have left is to go to Hell and get the Saint of Killers to kill the preacher. Fiore's up for going to Hell, because he's from Heaven and never been to Hell. One of the reasons DeBlanc took this job was to get out of Hell. The idea of going back petrifies him."

"They are the wrong people for this job," Brooke deliberately states. "They reason that if [the Saint of Killers] shoots Jesse, they will have another chance of getting Genesis back. He is their one and only last chance."

It is with reluctance that the angels ride a shuttle into Hell. "They've been brought together and have grown quite fond of each other," Brooke clarifies. "There's nothing like an adventure to bring people together, and they've certainly had that."

Much to Fiore's distress, only he makes it back. Says Catlin, "He truly does not give a shit anymore, he's so broken inside." And this is why Fiore turns to cabaret at the Mumbai Sky Tower, allowing himself to be killed over and over, in front of a live audience.

Brook's further thoughts on poor Fiore shed some light on the final situation he finds himself in: "Fiore doesn't like humans really. He thinks Jesse's an idiot, so Earth is tough for him. And DeBlanc was with him through all of it, so when he goes there's a friendship void that Cassidy fills. And if that means doing speedballs, eating ice cream and playing Frisbee, he'll take it. Once that's taken away though, it's too much for him, I think. Better to just stop."

It's useful at this point to hear Brooke's thoughts on working with Rogen, Goldberg and Catlin: "To be honest, the best thing about them was how sure they were that I was their guy. It gave me such confidence. I could relax and try stuff, which doesn't always happen — but when it does, and it works, it leads to 'Mumbai Sky Tower' which is THE MOST FUN I'VE EVER HAD ON FILM."

BELOW: The all-American setting of a late-night diner belies the strange conversation between two angels and a preacher with a gift.

ANGELIC APPARATUS

The angels DeBlanc (Anatol Yusef) and Fiore (Tom Brooke) are secretive and mysterious in their ways, and they carry several items of strange machinery. These gadgets were created for the show by Hex Mortis Studios, based in Georgia, United States. Both the music box used to try to draw out Genesis and the Heaven Phone are wonderful physical objects, with details worth poring over.

The music box is especially delightful because it is built from various parts salvaged from two antiques. Credit is also given to neighboring studio God Save the Queen fashions for providing the leather interior. Both devices look to have been handed down through many generations.

ABOVE: DeBlanc and Fiore do not understand why Jesse won't agree to their wishes.
BELOW: An old coffee can is not the sort of thing you'd expect to be able to keep an entity like Genesis in, but it worked in the past.

ABOVE: DeBlanc and Fiore contemplate the job at hand.
BELOW: In the end they join forces with Jesse when the seraphim turns up to complicate matters.

ANGELS VS VAN

Reinvigorated angels Fiore and DeBlanc return to All Saints Congregational Church, much to the confusion of Cassidy who'd only recently subjected both to horrific deaths. He doesn't recognize them at first and it's only after mowing them down with the church minibus that he realizes who they are. Cassidy concludes that they are clones. Close, but…never mind.

"Nothing can stop their mission, not even death," jokes Anatol Yusef (DeBlanc), and then outlines what is required from the actors for the scene: "We aren't being hit by a van, we just have to lay in the dust with green screen tights on and flailing limbs."

Makeup effects creator Howard Berger of KBM EFX explains how the resulting carnage is theatrically represented using body parts that are attached to the actor's costumes. Ruptured limbs appear to belong to the actors owing to them wearing green screen gloves and leggings. The fake arms and legs are made of latex skins backed with polyfoam. Armature wire runs through so that they can be positioned.

Mike Smithson, also of KBM EFX, says, "Most of these body parts will be under clothing, but for the carnage and trauma we're going to end up dressing and making it look realistic."

According to episode 3 director Scott Winant, multiple takes were required to combine the real actors with the fake dummies. "The dummies become real as soon as they're under the van, tumbling around. I will set up my cameras with the actors, then I remove them from those same setups, and have the van run through."

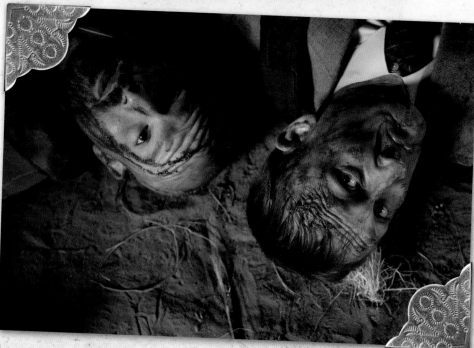

FAR RIGHT: *They look professional, don't they? Prepared. Equipped. But looks are often deceiving. All it took to take them down was a vampire in a van.*

Producer Seth Rogen states how the goal was to combine shots while making the scene visually interesting at the same time. For the stunt team, getting it right is not an exact science. They'd get the choreography down, then that would be changed too.

Characteristically buoyant on the subject, Joseph Gilgun says, "It's like a huge dance routine that you've got to work out in a matter of three or four days — if you're lucky. They make it fun."

In addition to the coordinating of special effects, stunts and the actual shooting of the scene, wardrobe faced an unusual challenge too.

Explains costume designer Karyn Wagner: "For a stunt like this, you have to consider costume items you can get eight to twelve copies of, because you need multiple takes for principal actors. You also have stunt performers who are standing in for them. The sets get dirty or destroyed. In this particular case, you have dummies that also need clothes."

CHURCH & CHAINSAW

"**A** big fight. With a lot of blood." Anatol Yusef's (DeBlanc) measured report of a standout scene in season 1, episode 1 'See' is to be admired. Equally, key special effects and make-up artist Mike Smithson of KNB EFX (*Breaking Bad, The Walking Dead*) is, umm, economical: "It doesn't go too well for two people."

Before we are clued in to DeBlanc and Fiore's collective incompetence, there's a chance that we might think they could mean serious business. Their grisly procedure on Jesse is interrupted by a lightly inebriated vampire, Cassidy, whom DeBlanc attempts to shoot dead. From the point where it's clear that this plainly has not worked, and with Cassidy gnawing on DeBlanc's leg, Fiore moves in with a spluttering chainsaw, swinging wildly, carving through empty air and chapel furniture.

"The scene goes from this very gentle lullaby, and becomes so violent!" Dominic Cooper (Jesse) chuckles, referring to DeBlanc being bludgeoned to death with a hymn book before Fiore loses an arm to the power-tool turned against him.

"We have this gag where Fiore gets his arm chopped off," Howard Berger, also of KNB EFX, details. "We've cast a hand that is in a 'holding a chainsaw' position, and this arm magnets on [to the actor]. We have tubing that is hooked up to one of our giant fire extinguishers. The tubing is rigged inside [the arm], and I notched it all so that blood would spray out. The arm stays attached to the

ABOVE, RIGHT AND BELOW: *When singing fails, move to dismemberment.*

"Get away from him now, you filthy little gobshites!"

Cass

ABOVE: Hubris strikes Cassidy when the pair he thought had come for him put a bullet in his torso. But he doesn't stay down for long...

BELOW: The Archangel Gabriel carried a sword. Our Fiore favors a chainsaw.

ABOVE: As stated earlier, the eyebrows do a lot of work.

BELOW AND ABOVE RIGHT: All Saints Church, holy place, house of God, battlefield.

ABOVE: *Cas, Fiore's arm and the chainsaw that did the damage.*

chainsaw..." SFX coordinator Daniel Holt explains that there were three remote control components in the chainsaw that allowed it to creep slowly along the floor – towards the comatose Jesse.

According to executive producer Seth Rogen, "Weeks and weeks of prep go into a fight. But...a chainsaw fight?" Says co-executive Evan Goldberg, "It's crazy. Our stunt coordinator John Koyama makes little movies of it which we can discuss and go over together."

"Once we lock something in, we'll then train the actors and teach them the fight and the choreography," Koyama outlines. "It's one thing to do it with our team, but it's another when the actors come in because they bring their characters with them. It's like a recipe, and they put the final little spices and touches into it."

In other words, shooting *Preacher* scenes isn't so simple, especially when they are difficult to begin with.

BELOW: *A mortal fight with two angels only a day or so after jumping out of a plane without a parachute. Welcome to the life of this particular vampire.*

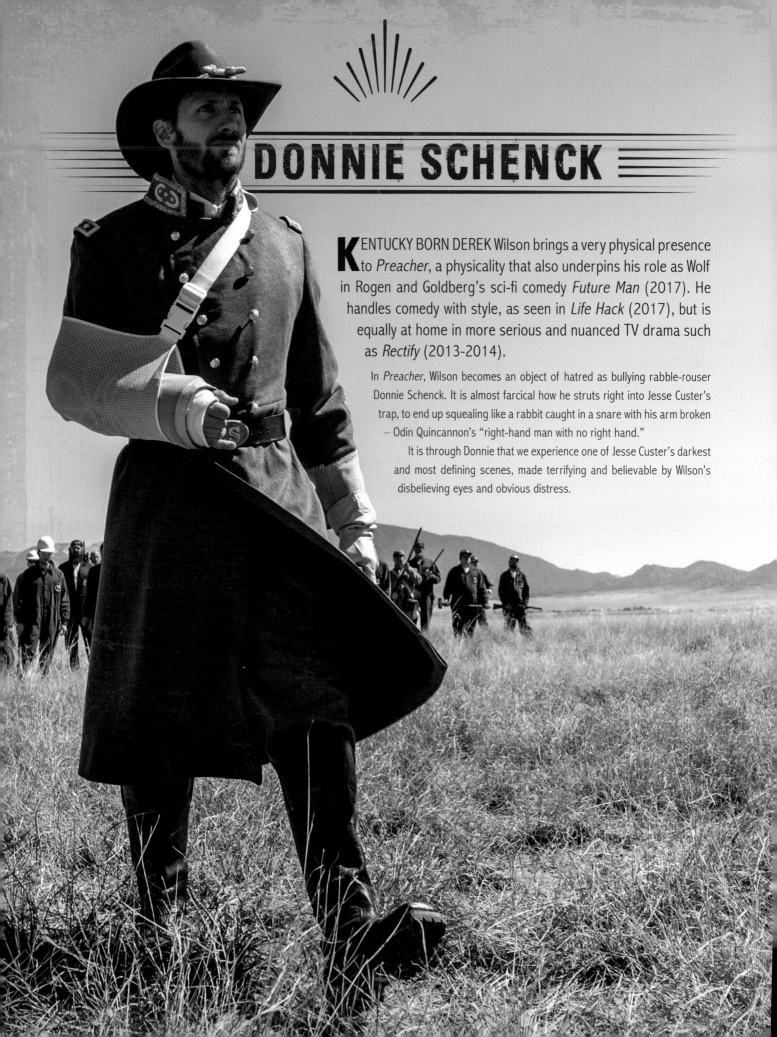

DONNIE SCHENCK

KENTUCKY BORN DEREK Wilson brings a very physical presence to *Preacher*, a physicality that also underpins his role as Wolf in Rogen and Goldberg's sci-fi comedy *Future Man* (2017). He handles comedy with style, as seen in *Life Hack* (2017), but is equally at home in more serious and nuanced TV drama such as *Rectify* (2013-2014).

In *Preacher*, Wilson becomes an object of hatred as bullying rabble-rouser Donnie Schenck. It is almost farcical how he struts right into Jesse Custer's trap, to end up squealing like a rabbit caught in a snare with his arm broken — Odin Quincannon's "right-hand man with no right hand."

It is through Donnie that we experience one of Jesse Custer's darkest and most defining scenes, made terrifying and believable by Wilson's disbelieving eyes and obvious distress.

That moment occurs in the gas station restroom where Donnie confronts Jesse with a loaded gun, confident that he has the troublesome preacher at his mercy. He is then astonished to find himself redirecting the gun into his own mouth with the hammer fully cocked.

From Wilson's point of view, "I think in that moment [Jesse] realizes that this power could be used for something much grander. It's unbelievable. Donnie's whimpering on a toilet with a gun in his mouth. He's beaten. He doesn't need to die. The thing that that sets up is now Donnie — a very dangerous person, an unhinged person — knows about this power."

Donnie doesn't retreat with his tail between his legs. Instead he volunteers to lead the charge against Jesse to claim the local church and its land for Quincannon. Observes Evan Goldberg, "Donnie's willing to go to any length. I think to him, at this point, it's better dead than not redeemed."

Speaking in admiration for his own character's solution to the obstacle posed by Genesis, not to mention the surprising effectiveness with which Jesse is holding his ground, Wilson states, "Donnie sees that this siege isn't working. He's going to have to come up with something else. And he does. And it's brilliant. And it works. He becomes the hero of this episode."

BELOW: *A grotty gas station restroom is the scene of this turning of the tables. Donnie thinks he's got the drop on Jesse, but he's a luckless character and is put in his place.*

BETSY SCHENCK

The first we hear of Betsy Schenck is through the pleas of her young son, Chris, who is hopeful that his preacher will teach his dad a painful lesson and end what we presume is serial abuse. Actually, as Donnie Schenck later informs his boy, grown-up life can get a little complicated. He need not worry, and the audience can afford a wry smile on account of the little guy.

Actress Jamie Anne Allman (*The Notebook, The Killing*) plays the part brilliantly, giving the impression of somebody who may need help, before announcing the kinky truth behind she and Donnie's bedroom affairs. We're not quite sure if we hear her correctly the first time. It dawns on us while that same realization comes snaking into Jesse's voice. "No. No, no, no."

BELOW: *Although their relationship begins with violence, Jesse's actions teach Donnie that he is not a killer, and that he should let God into his heart.*

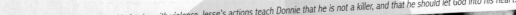

A PREACHER WALKS INTO A BAR

Fight coordinator Jeff Imada (*The Bourne Ultimatum, Iron Man 2*) worked alongside Seth Rogen, Sam Catlin and Evan Goldberg to provide insight into Jesse Custer that almost no other scene could so elegantly achieve.

Recalls Dominic Cooper, "You're so focused in fight scenes, trying to look scary and strong. Actually, Seth said don't do any of that. After learning the choreography of the fight, just smile your way through it." While Cooper was rehearsing the moves between shoots, Rogen suggested that he behave as though shadow boxing, or play-fighting with kids coming at him — smacking their hands out of the way, or hitting them on the face. This is the attitude that the producers wanted for Jesse when going up against Donnie Schenck

and his men.

"We did a few fight scenes in some of our other stuff that were pretty good," says Rogen. "But I think the pilot of *Preacher* was the first time we did a fight scene and I was like, 'those are pretty good fight scenes on the grand scale of fight scenes!'"

For the final payoff, where Jesse fractures Donnie's forearm, practical effects were used that were so effective they grossed out Rogen and those who hadn't seen them in action.

A device was strapped to actor Derek Wilson's arm, requiring only a slight nudge to trigger. The fake bone popped out, right before Wilson's disbelieving eyes ("Almost done, Sheriff"). We know then exactly what kind of preacher we are dealing with.

BELOW: *Donnie's back from re-fighting the Civil War, so he can handle the preacher who got into his business, right? Right?*

"You'd hear a noise. A high-pitched, kind of bunny-in-a-bear-trap sound. You'll know it when it comes 'cause you're the one who'll be making it."

Jesse

YOUNG JESSE

AMID THE MANY reasons we find to celebrate *Preacher*, the revelatory performances of the actors who played Tulip and Jesse as kids are particularly special. Ashley Aufderheide and Dominic Ruggieri so powerfully grasp their respective roles as Tulip and Jesse that we perceive in them echoes of their trials during the adult couple's scenes. We stare through the same eyes into troubled hearts unchanged.

Dominic Cooper carefully examines Jesse and Tulip's younger selves: "There's no one more important to each of them than the other. They are the center of one another's world. All of Jesse's decisions revolve around what happened to them as children."

Unsurprisingly, Aufderheide and Ruggieri are cheerful and spirited individuals off-screen, but their portrayals of key events to camera are astounding. "I'm supposed to play a really tough character, so I have to be really tough," laughs Aufderheide, before hitting the nail on the head regarding a pivotal scene. "I think John Custer takes me away because I'm an O'Hare."

She is talking about the heartrending incident where the Department of Human Services take Tulip away, at John Custer's behest. "It's a pretty intense scene," explains Ruggieri. "John Custer is taking away my bestest friend ever, in the whole world. My hand swelled up, because of banging on the car so much [during takes]. [Michael Morris, episode director] gave me a lot of direction in this scene. I know he wanted it to be very intense. I started out a little quiet, but I got more intense."

One of the writers for episode 6 'He Gone' is Mary Laws. "We're fortunate because we've got two really smart kids. It's been sort of breezy so far," Laws said during production.

Nathan Darrow, who plays John Custer, Jesse's father, shows similar gratitude toward his youthful collaborators. "The most you

ABOVE: *The happy smiles of the actors who play young Jesse and Tulip belie the intensity of the scenes they play.*

want from an actor you're working with is that they are available and present to what is happening in the scene. Dominic blew me away. I'm still evaluating it myself, thinking 'I want more of that. I'm gonna steal that'."

Because Aufderheide is so credible as Tulip when she is driven away — silently staring ahead while Jesse frantically gives chase — we can believe that Jesse then goes to his room to pray for his father's death. Upon the foundation of Jesse's subsequent guilt, of bearing witness to his father's gruesome departure from this world, Garth Ennis erected the story of *Preacher*.

Episode 6 of season 1 is remarkable because, almost without warning, it yanks away the veil between the present and the past in such a powerful a manner.

BELOW: *This is a scene that changes Jesse's life forever: the death of his father, for which he blames himself.*

ODIN QUINCANNON

A CADEMY AWARD NOMINATED for performances in *Little Children* (2006) and *Lincoln* (2012), and with chilling appearances in *Nightmare on Elm Street* and *Shutter Island* (both in 2010), Jackie Earle Haley brings gravitas to his role as unscrupulous meat baron Odin Quincannon.

Having played *Nightmare on Elm Street*'s Freddie Kreuger and *Shutter Island*'s repeat offender George Noyce, Haley is well versed in the ways of dark determination. Odin's presence haunts Annville County from the brown and bleak office in the 125-year-old slaughterhouse, Quincannon Meat & Power.

Showrunner Sam Catlin sets the scene, "While Jesse has been away from this town, Odin Quincannon has become sort of the

"Today we answer mankind's most pressing question. Namely... what the Hell's going on?"

Odin

ultimate white whale of sin. He's a professed atheist. He's also the most powerful man in town. He basically runs Annville. Jesse's trying to coax Odin to come to church just this one Sunday. For Jesse, he's the ultimate challenge: 'If I can show the town that I can bring Odin Quincannon to God, then everyone else will follow.'"

It appears an impossible task. Quincannon suffered the death of his entire family on a ski trip, after which he bewilderedly receives their broken bodies in crudely constructed crates. Comments Haley, "He starts to tear into their bodies, in search of their souls. Not only was there not a God, he saw that we are nothing but meat."

"For Odin it was a complete loss of faith," remarks Evan Goldberg. "He did the right things: he made a family; he's wealthy, successful; he's hard working. And all that's gone."

"As a result of that," Catlin summarizes, "Quincannon made a scientific calculation that there is no God. He becomes a staunch, rabid atheist."

Undeterred by his father's words from long ago ("Some people just can't be saved"), Jesse believes that now he has Genesis he can work some kind of miracle on Quincannon. This is all the more remarkable — especially given his boyhood memory of Quincannon clutching the entrails of an animal in one hand and those of his daughter in the other, lamenting the fact that he cannot tell them apart.

ABOVE: *Odin Quincannon listens to the sound of dying cattle as if it's a symphony.*

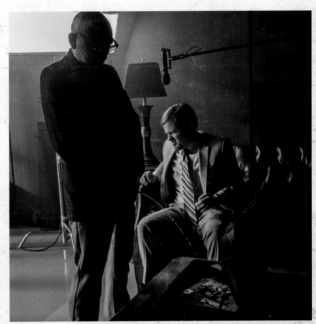

ABOVE: *Odin Quincannon is also not a man burdened by inhibition.*

ABOVE: *Odin Quincannon's office — a place dense with dark thoughts and darker deeds.*

In the present day, Jesse gambles on turning things around for the decrepit businessman. But before making Quincannon an offer even he can't refuse, he decides to test the water. As Catlin explains, "Jesse prods him and asks him, 'What about Hell? Aren't you worried about Hell?' But Odin turns the tables on Jesse. 'I'm not the one that's worried about Hell, you're the one that's worried about Hell.'

And that's the turn of the scene."

Even after Jesse succeeds, through Genesis, in commanding Quincannon to "serve God", the shocking outcome reveals who Quincannon's master truly is. As consulting producer Craig Rosenberg makes clear, "Odin's idea of serving his god is to slaughter his rivals."

ABOVE: Odin: "The only true God, the only real God, is the God of Meat."

ABOVE: Odin to Jesse: "You know the rules. I don't talk about how my meat gets made. You don't talk about your magic man in the sky."

BELOW: Odin is forced to change his views about God again. Note that the bearded vision is reflected in Odin's glasses.

BLOODY BUSINESS

eason 1, episode 4 'South Will Rise Again' comes to an end with a calm and cozy meeting between Odin Quincannon and four organic food producers. We're not intended to have a single clue about what will transpire. Although, admittedly, this is Odin Quincannon we're talking about.

Co-executive producer Michael Slovis (*Fringe*, *Breaking Bad*) says of the closing minutes, "We play the beginning of it very casually and informally. There is nothing at the beginning of the scene that gives away what happens at the end." Odin cordially addresses the female Green Acre executive as "young lady", serving her a drink

shortly before shooting her dead. She is the second to last victim, gawking in horror at Odin's shotgun.

The last guy apologizes for being late, and is dropped by Odin before he can enter the door.

"We've used heightened reality, so we produce more blood than you would normally have in real life," Slovis declares. "When somebody gets shot on TV and the stunt performers get blown back, well, that doesn't happen in real life. In real life people who are shot just drop."

Says Ricky Mabe (Miles Person), "When I got to reading that

BELOW: *What begins as an ordinary business meeting takes an unexpected turn.*

ABOVE: *At least he got a snifter of brandy before he took a shotgun blast to the chest.*

part, I literally got some saliva on the page because my mouth was so agape. It's amazing how much fear can be packed into a tight man." Mabe's quizzical expression as he internalizes the scene is hard to read.

"I would imagine, in Miles' head, there's not only shock, but great disappointment," laughs Slovis.

EMILY WOODROW

AFTER PORTRAYING A defiant Marian in *Robin Hood* (BBC, 2006-2009), British actress Lucy Griffiths topped Cassidy's track record as a 345-year-old vampire as Nora in *True Blood* (2012-2013). In *Preacher*, it's Griffiths' talent for showing characters keeping a tight lid on their feelings before betraying their truest intentions with a glance that proves ideal for single-mother and helper at the church, Emily.

In season 1, Emily's shrewd eye-view guides audience perception of Jesse throughout suspicious goings-on. She is a pillar of the old community, dedicated to her young family, available, though not at all desperate — a fact overlooked by cloying suitor Mayor Miles Person.

> "Since when did people require Frappuccinos to come to church?"
>
> Emily

ABOVE: *Emily serves breakfast food at the Flavor Station, but chargilled vampires need live sustenance, either animal...or mayor.*

Inspired by Tulip's unwavering resolve (Emily: "Where are you going?" Tulip: "I'm going to kill a man in Albuquerque."), Emily musters the courage to take matters into her own hands. Says Griffiths, "Tulip's a doer. She makes her wishes, or desires, into reality. Miles is pushy, demanding attention. He interferes. Emily relates to the notion of being trapped."

As Ruth Negga comments, "It awakens an instinct to take control of her own life." And, on the subject of being a role model of sorts for Emily, "Tulip feels deeply allied towards people who have been treated unfairly. She feels a deep need to speak for the voiceless."

"[Emily] feels completely powerless," explains Griffiths. "And the only thing that she can do is to get rid of him." Specifically, Emily feeds Miles to the recuperating, repugnant and very hungry Cassidy.

Concludes showrunner Sam Catlin, "By killing Miles, she sort-of comes alive herself."

"If a bunch of guys
turned up and tried to
take my home I'd shoot
at them too."

Emily

INSET ABOVE: *Although it's never stated explicitly, we think Emily cares deeply for Jesse, and perhaps in this moment she's wishing he'd move a bit closer.*

ABOVE: *Emily to Tulip: "You just broke my kid's art thing, so yeah, nice job."*

RIGHT: *The 'art thing'.*

ABOVE: *Tulip makes amends.*

MAYOR MILES PERSON

RICKY MABE (PRONOUNCED 'maybe') previously crossed paths with director Seth Rogen when they worked together on *Zack and Miri Make a Porno* (2008). Mabe has appeared in numerous light-hearted roles throughout his career, his *joie de vivre* shining through children's heroes Timmy Tibble in *Arthur* (1996-2000) and Stig in *Pig City* (2002) before we got to see him as the mayor of Annville.

> "Sometimes what's legal isn't as important as what's right. Sometimes sacrifices have to be made."
>
> Mayor Person

For *Preacher*, Mabe's youthful good looks — a useful asset for other roles, serious or silly — make us simultaneously sympathetic and mistrustful of his intentions.

The Canadian received a Golden Maple Award for appearing as an extraordinarily nice guy opposite David Krumholtz's zany grandma on IFC's comedy *Gigi Does It*, which he co-wrote and produced. As Annville mayor, Miles Person, Mabe becomes Odin Quincannon's unwitting conspirator, while elsewhere he attempts to woo an apparently vulnerable single mom, Emily. Though we do feel sorry for Miles, we are all rooting for Emily when she introduces him to Cassidy.

"When I get to go to work and see people get decapitated, get shot right through the chest — that's so far from my real life, I revert back to being a ten-year-old boy playing with G.I. Joe," says Mabe about being involved with the most extreme content that *Preacher* has to offer.

BELOW: *The Mayor and the mascot.*

CARLOS & THE BANK RAID

In this vital flashback scene we see Jesse and Tulip in a previous life, both criminals and having a terrific time.

While our latter-day Bonnie & Clyde are goofing around in the vault of First Perpetual Bank, Carlos (Desmin Borges) distracts passers-by outside the main door. We know what's coming, and it hurts, but the veil pulled back on the backstory to the lovers' most painful memory is something we simply cannot pull ourselves away from. Almost out of respect for the loss that is just around the corner, as though facing the pain of it ourselves.

Jesse and Tulip are clearly different. They are happy, unaware of how this simple fact will turn Carlos against them. Beforehand we see Carlos' visible discomfort at the couple's flirtatious behavior. It's like there's nothing to it — the job, and them being so close.

For the audience, this is all a set up for the bleakest of moments in Jesse and Tulip's lives. Carlos betrays his accomplices by freeing a security guard held prisoner in the bank, who Jesse eventually guns down. As Carlos screeches from the alley in the getaway car, Tulip crouches over and, shivering, whispers to Jesse, "the baby." We feel devastated.

BELOW: *Jesse and Tulip in earlier, happier and more criminal times, doing what they do best.*

BELOW AND RIGHT: *"Fun's over, Custer. Now the pain begins."*

BELOW: Carlos' decision to betray his partners seems like a spur of the moment decision based on spite — Jesse and Tulip are happy, and he is not.

ABOVE: *Realization dawns that Carlos has betrayed them. Can Tulip have any idea as to why? And worse, so much worse, is about to happen...*

Fast forward to the present day, where Tulip has just confronted Jesse with the task of finishing the job on Carlos. "For Tulip, revenge isn't only an option, it's the *only* option," says Ruth Negga. "She needs Jesse to do it with her, to share her anger and to share her pain."

"You actually think she's killed him off the bat," explains Evan Goldberg, "but she has something a little more specific in mind." The audience does not know what to expect.

After some conflict ("Carlos is a reminder of this intolerable pain that he can't deal with," discloses Dominic Cooper) Jesse is prepared

to go through with killing Carlos, who is lying bound and gagged in the trunk of Tulip's car. However, Tulip steps in before it is done.

"Killing Carlos isn't going to make Tulip less sad," Negga imparts. In the scene, Tulip tells Jesse, "That's the most beautiful thing anyone's ever done for me," concluding that, "It wouldn't make a difference. It's the thought, okay? That's what counts."

When describing the conclusion to the scene Goldberg is delightfully off-hand, summarizing: "They decide to beat the shit out of him, and then tell him to fuck off forever."

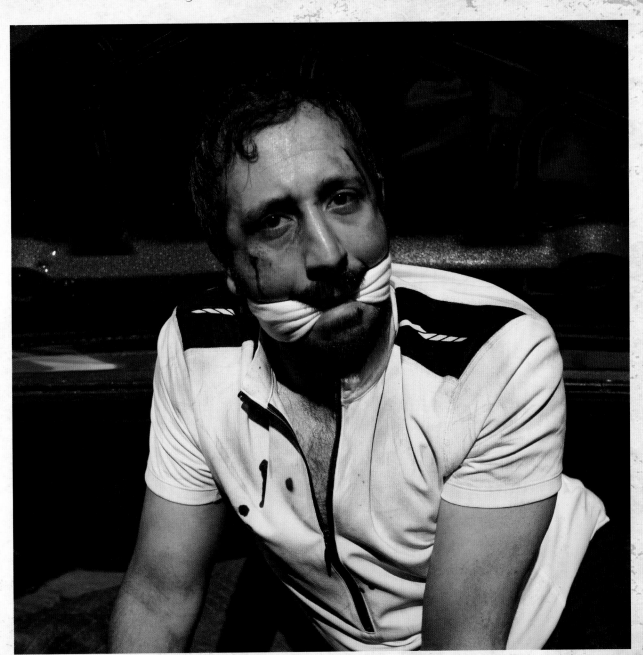

ABOVE: Carlos' questionable taste in leasure-wear, plus gag.

BELOW: Carlos must have expected the worst when his erstwhile partners caught up with him. In the end, it could have been worse.

ASSAULT ON ALL SAINTS

Jesse lost his bet with Odin, who did not convert to Christianity even after being ordered by Genesis to serve God. Thus emboldened, the belligerent businessman hurries to have Jesse sign over his father's land, to which our pugnacious preacher flat out refuses.

A spectacular stand-off ensues as Odin brings an army of meat men to tear down All Saints. Jesse prepares to defend. What happens next starts out surprising, ends up uncomfortable.

Producer Matt Tauber has the gist: "Jesse's in an interesting spot here. He's running on fumes, really. He's not shooting to kill.

He's just kind of keeping everything at bay. We had to find really fun ways of him taking Odin's men down without causing any casualties. We've got a lot of great stunts in this scene."

"Nobody expected Jesse's fight back to be as successful as it is," says Derek Wilson (Donnie Schenck) "As soon as I saw all the stunt guys say, 'Yeah, I'll take some ear plugs', I was like, 'Yeah, I'm gonna do what they do'."

Special effects coordinator Daniel Holt (*Breaking Bad*, *Let Me In*) talks us through the stages. "We've got a baseball bat that blows up.

ABOVE: *"When you hear the battle cry, I want y'all to race forward and try real hard not to get your penises shot off."*

That had an explosive inside of it. We waited for the director's cue, and when the time was right we blew it [to make it look like Jesse has shot it].

"We've got a meat man who gets his helmet shot off, and that goes into another meat man's face. We had a guy off camera and ran a line through the hardhat through his shirt.

"We've got a machete being shot out of a guy's hand. And then we also built a rig for a guy for a 'reveal' that has the machete sticking out of his shoulder. We yanked the machete from our actor, then we had our stunt man take the hit."

Tait Fletcher is the stuntman in question, who explains that the embedded metal machete required the SFX team to make a form and a mold, which is then attached to his harness.

Holt continues step by step through the second most memorable event that occurs: "We didn't want a huge explosion when Jesse throws a Molotov cocktail out the window and hits a bulldozer because this is just a small bottle filled with some sort of oil. We placed charges on the front of the bulldozer, right where the actual impact would happen. The stuntman driving the bulldozer was gelled up for protection, and we tested the fireball several times so we didn't get him caught on fire. We did have a secondary explosion that's supposed to show the motor going up after the bulldozer catches fire. We put in some big aftermath smoke for Clive to come through in the end."

We owe Clive, played by Alex Knight, the last word here. "I think what Jesse does to Clive certainly stops him, to say the least. It stops a lot of the men.

"It strikes a certain fear."

VAMPIRE CASSIDY

You could argue that this scene belongs to Emily (Lucy Griffiths), given the apparently premeditated decision she makes. However, Miles Person (Ricky Mabe) being fed to Cassidy (Joseph Gilgun) is also memorable because, well, it's so gross.

Key special effects make-up artist Mike Smithson of KNB EFX worked with his crew to conjure a few minutes of screen time that haunted mealtimes for maybe a month. Here, Mike explains the process behind Cassidy's transformation:

"Cassidy has third- and fourth-degree burns all over his body. We had a partial burn suit on him, with arm appliances and facial appliances. We also had some sparse hair-pieces.

"We do look at forensic photographs in order to get the textures and coloration right. James (Rohland) and I did a three-quarter live cast on Joe, who was a great sport about it. In this particular make-up Joe can eat, smoke and drink coffee."

According to Gilgun the half-body prosthetic "takes four to five hours to get on, forty-five minutes to get off, but it's worth it. It makes my job really easy." As for his ravenous performance, Gilgun quips, "Every now and again someone needs eating."

Ricky Mabe comments that Cassidy/Joe "looks incredible, he looks disgusting. These clumps of hair all over him, this peeling skin." Referring back to Gilgun's comments about making his job

BELOW: *It's shocking to see Cass in this feral, bloodthirsty state.*

"You should go Preacher. It's not safe for you here."

Cass

ABOVE: *Delivered by Emily.*

ABOVE: *Eaten by Cass.*

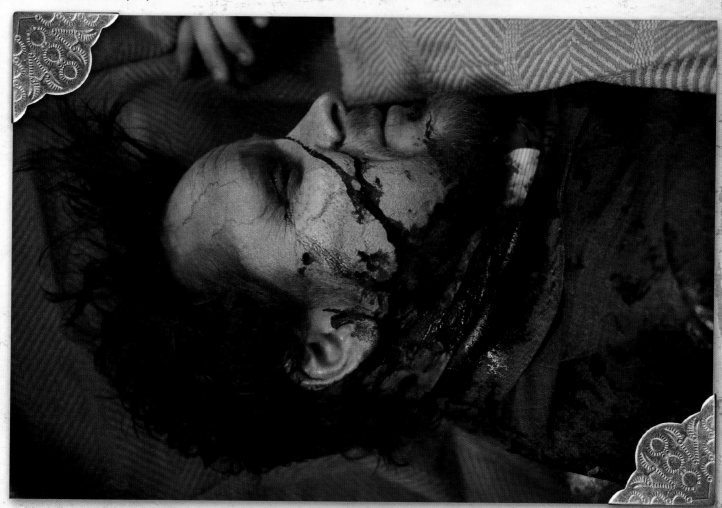

ABOVE: *Impressive make-up effects show the sad fate of Mayor Miles Person. Look, his hair's all mussed up.*

easier, Mabe said vampire Cassidy's unnerving presence also aided his performance.

"I'm so glad they went with the practical effects make-up," says Mabe, "because it's there; it's in the room, it's tangible. It helps me as an actor get to a real place because I see it in front of me. I think this is my absolute favorite way to go. I was so glad when I read in the script that that's how Miles is taken out. It's too bad, because he's unbearably handsome."

BATTLE ROYALE

Season 1, episode 5 'Sundowner' is a supreme example of the show's knack for introducing violent and extremely bloody chaos from an apparent state of calm. DeBlanc and Fiore's confrontation with Susan the seraphim at the Sundowner Motel starts with a scuffle we could never predict, leading to scenes that audiences will not soon forget.

"I'm not sure that there's ever been anything like it on TV before," declares Anatol Yusef (DeBlanc). "The fight goes on for a very, very long time and it takes a while to restrain her."

Restraint is the only way to halt Susan's relentless onslaught, because killing her only causes her to "reinvigorate". The tiny motel room soon gets packed as the three celestial beings die repeatedly, reinvigorating each time, carpeting the floor with blood-soaked corpses.

It seems as though this spectacular gore-fest could last forever, as it rages into the night.

"That changes the whole dynamic of how you tell a story, because you never have a beginning, middle and end of the fight. You have an ongoing fight," says Guillermo Navarro, director of episode 5.

Explains stunt coordinator John Koyama, "The characters are killed, but their body stays and their form comes back to life again. You have to use the environment. We really wanted to concentrate on

BELOW: *A fight that could go on forever...*

SERAPHIM

Actress and stunt performer Juliana Potter is simply ferocious as Susan, and there may never be a sequence to top the arrival of her near unstoppable seraphim. "Though she be but little, she is fierce," to quote Potter, quoting Shakespeare, via Twitter. Role models, kids. Role models.

Something we did not cover is Potter's spooky exit after convincing Hugo Root to put her out of her limbless misery.

Her sneaking away in the background, while Root strangles the life out of her broken body, is brilliant. Moreover, it's an intelligent set-up for the closing seconds of season 1, where the apparently indestructible Susan lurches through the reeking wreck that once was Annville, before being one-shotted by the Saint of Killers.

But while she lasted, she was little yet fierce.

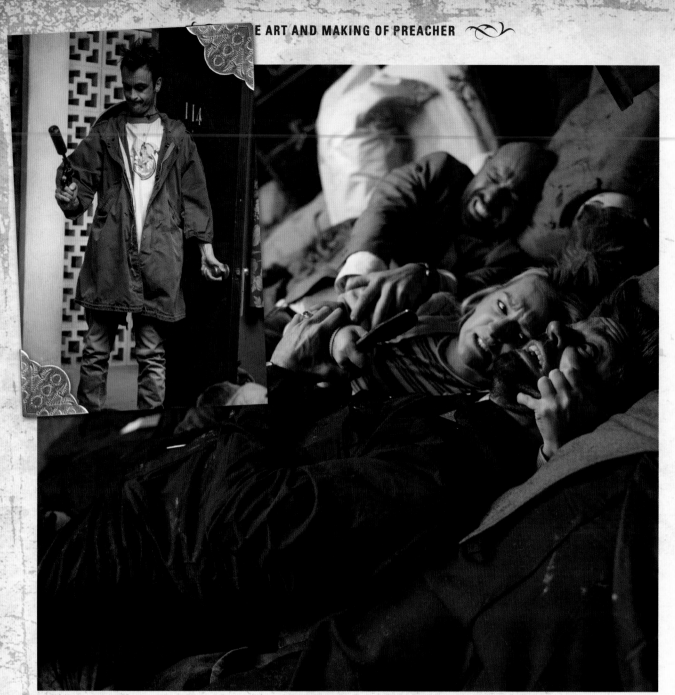

ABOVE: *This crazy scene demanded total commitment and a lot of energy from everyone involved.*

the bodies piling up. Now those can be obstacles. It looks sloppy, it looks messy, it looks dirty."

Key to the surprising humor of the motel scene is the seraphim's diminutive size in relation to everybody else. Having said that, writer Nick Towne mentions how "we didn't want how small she was to be too much of a gag, but we definitely wanted it to be referenced."

As actress Juliana Potter describes, "Most of the time my height – 4'9" – is used in the stunt industry as niche. It's not typical that I'm fighting really tall people or men. Now I'm this blood-gutsing gore fighter. Whenever I fight tall people, they're like, 'God, my legs are killing me.' It's actually really fun to be my own character, and kick

the living crap out of the main characters. I came in here with pads on, gloves on, ready to fight."

"That whole experience was exciting," smiles Dominic Cooper (Jesse). "We had a lot of different fight sequences to learn. It was great fun to shoot that scene."

"It's outrageous and fun, with moments of utter lunacy," concurs Tom Brooke (Fiore).

"Koyama is just a straight-up bad-ass coordinator and a bad-ass fighter," enthuses Potter. "He wants his fighting to really speak to an audience. To have a stunt coordinator there by your side, that's a good stunt coordinator. Practice makes…not necessarily perfect, but it does make things better; makes things way more safe."

ABOVE AND BELOW: *This scene needed a lot of preparation, practice and carefully placed dummies.*

METHANE CONTROL ROOM

Annville, Jesse's home town, is built upon a literal river of crap. Manure collected from the livestock at Quincannon Meat & Power slaughterhouse has been gathering in vats beneath the ground to power a Methane-Electro Reactor. It is extremely unpleasant, exceedingly hazardous, and the responsibility of one man to ensure the whole thing does not explode.

We know him as Pappy, the sex-starved monitor whose job seems to entail nothing much more than releasing pressure when a valve reading reaches critical. Pappy is another fine example of passing incident that has no immediate consequence, but catches up with you further down the line. Those in the audience paying closest attention to *Preacher* through season 1 noticed something unusual that seemed linked to Pappy; a pipe poking out of the ground close to All Saint's Congregational Church, occasionally spewing gas of some kind.

It's funny how much we get to know and later suspect about Pappy from just a few lines of dialogue, plus some creative thought regarding the inevitable destruction of All Saint's. A phone call to his wife ending in affectionate resignation. We genuinely feel for him.

In the season 1 grand finale, it becomes clear that Pappy had sought to assuage a particular urge, inviting a mysterious BDSM partner to play away from home. Pappy clearly had a great time, and is seen passed out in the foreground while methane pressure rises out of control. Possibly, Pappy is already dead but this is soon to become an irrelevance.

BELOW: *Through the window on the left is the vast reservoir of manure from Quincannon's slaughterhouse. Quite a view for Pappy. No wonder he needs other kinds of stimulation.*

ABOVE: *The methane control room set design, with its drab color and all those dials, relays and quivering needles has a real 1960s vibe.*

NEW ORLEANS

The Big Easy is portrayed more along the lines of The Big Sleazy in season 2. One early scene there involves a man in a dog suit, not to mention the hiring of prostitutes by Cassidy to amuse Denis, or to mistakenly attend to Herr Starr's introspective urge. In the intro to each episode, New Orleans lives up to its billing as the City that Care Forgot; the phrase coined by hotel owner Alfred S. Amer in 1910. A perpetual carnival that spills from the streets into smoke-filled bars — a party spirit that contrasts with Tulip's furtive glances, which so unsettle Cassidy.

However, it is New Orleans' proud ownership of the Birthplace of Jazz mantle that directly serves the narrative. It's apparently where God himself headed, in search of his passions, although leading Jesse and his entourage on what seems to be a wild goose chase. Knowing this, Grail operatives FJ Hoover and Lara Featherstone pose

BELOW: *Jesse arrives in New Orleans with a job to do: find God. Too bad if it involves visiting every Jazz club in the city.*

"The plan is simple: find God."
Jesse

as bar tender and lounge singer respectively to lead Jesse astray, a ruse that allows them to confirm Jesse's power.

The headiness of the town disrupts almost all sense of certainty, allowing plot twists such as Tulip's previous marriage to Viktor to catch us unawares, and the revelation that a French-speaking old man called Denis is in fact Cassidy's estranged son. Through New Orleans, the road trip mentality takes off, with Cassidy taking his opportunity to express true feelings toward Tulip, while Jesse starts to believe in his own legend — an opportunity that's seized upon by Herr Starr.

BELOW: *Jesse's odyssey to find God takes him to the best dives in New Orleans.*

BELOW: *Jesse has a quiet drink on his quest to find God. And in the background is Lara Featherstone, no doubt with an eye on her quarry.*

THE ANGEL & THE VAMPIRE

By the time we reach 'Mumbai Sky Tower' (season 2, episode 2), strange is the new normal. The brief yet special relationship that blossoms between vampire Cassidy and angel Fiore is hilarious on the one hand, and beautiful on the other. It's also quite dastardly on the vampire's part, because he guarantees to Jesse and Tulip that he'll gain Fiore's trust inside of two hours and forty-five minutes.

The trio is attempting to stop the relentless pursuit of the Saint of Killers. Apparently Fiore can call him off, but he staunchly refuses. Indignant Fiore even dares Jesse to use Genesis: "Go on then. Make me. Use it. Watch what happens."

Joseph Gilgun, Cassidy, imparts his character's view of the episode, "This guy Fiore just needs a pal. If anything, he needs a blowout. Every now and again, we go out, we get drunk, we forget

BELOW: *A quiet moment of bathing and comic reading for our new friends.*

ABOVE: *Fiore's relationship with Cass is brief but eventful.*

what we've said the night before, it's all a bit of a nightmare. But for some reason it does us the world of good." Everything within this hazy story sequence is magnificently portrayed.

This short dialogue on the matter, between producers Goldberg and Rogen is to be savored:

Evan: "Cass believes that he can convince Fiore to help them in their mission and provide them with some information —"

Seth: [interrupting] "He's mostly just manipulating him, I think."

Evan: "I mean, that's a dark way to look at it. I think he manipulated him, *while* being his friend."

Seth: "Yeah, that's true."

HURT LOCKER

The subversive New Orleans gun club holds a trance-like allure for Tulip after her near-death encounter with the Saint of Killers. We first step into the bar with Jesse, Tulip and Cassidy in season 2, episode 7, 'Pig'; initially a cash-raising ruse. "The big ones pay more, right?"

As a venue, there's nothing much to it: a well-stocked bar, with a stenciled sign, a table, some guns and a box of cash. Oh, and some rowdy dudes that our heroes plan to impress. With Cassidy as guinea pig, and Tulip posing as his convivial partner — outspoken against an intervening holy man (Jesse) to complete the confidence trick — our first taste of Hurt Locker is a humorous one. The most concern we have at this stage is for Cass, flat on his ass with a lingering kiss from Tulip on his lips adding to some temporary pain.

Hurt Locker takes on a much darker purpose later this same episode, likely timed so that the audience doesn't soon forget the lighter-hearted Tulip that enjoyed manipulating a crowd. Haunted by vivid nightmares, Tulip chooses to internalize the emotional agony and subject her body to punishment, taking body shots through a Kevlar vest, staring death in the face.

We are aware of Tulip's PTSD ritual while her friends are kept in the dark. In a way, knowing something secret about one of the key characters, and we can see the signs, wondering if somebody — Cassidy? — might recognize that something is wrong, feels intensely personal.

ABOVE AND BELOW: *Strange and intense goings-on occur behind the doors of the Hurt Locker.*

ABOVE AND ABOVE RIGHT: *The patrons of the Hurt Locker know and love their guns.*

ABOVE AND BELOW: *A kiss and crossed fingers are no protection against bullets, but Cass puts himself in harm's way anyway.*

SAINT OF KILLERS

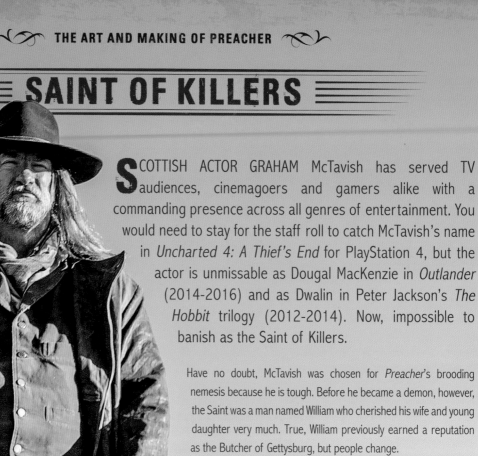

SCOTTISH ACTOR GRAHAM McTavish has served TV audiences, cinemagoers and gamers alike with a commanding presence across all genres of entertainment. You would need to stay for the staff roll to catch McTavish's name in *Uncharted 4: A Thief's End* for PlayStation 4, but the actor is unmissable as Dougal MacKenzie in *Outlander* (2014-2016) and as Dwalin in Peter Jackson's *The Hobbit* trilogy (2012-2014). Now, impossible to banish as the Saint of Killers.

Have no doubt, McTavish was chosen for *Preacher*'s brooding nemesis because he is tough. Before he became a demon, however, the Saint was a man named William who cherished his wife and young daughter very much. True, William previously earned a reputation as the Butcher of Gettysburg, but people change.

The past, however, does not forget, and karma sure came calling at the worst possible time in the godforsaken town named Ratwater. You know this story, and how it ends (not well). McTavish had all of the above reference points to absorb for his character's portrayal, which exudes the unbearable pain and an unquenchable thirst for bloody revenge.

"I was a huge fan of Garth and Steve's graphic novels long before the TV show happened," says McTavish. "When I heard about Seth and Evan producing I desperately wanted to be involved. And

ABOVE: *The Saint is dressed and equipped to intimidate, but it's those burning eyes that hold the most power.*

then when they asked me to talk about playing the Saint I was over the moon. I felt a huge responsibility to the fans (being one myself) to be true to the spirit of the Saint. When I donned that duster coat, and strapped on the .44 Walker Colts I felt the literal weight of the character and I kept saying to myself, 'Don't fuck this up!'"

"There's something so chilling about the Saint of Killers, even when you're on set with him," says Ruth Negga (Tulip), who is lifted off her feet and throttled by the fiend. "This is a man who has no light. Nothing there. How do you figure out what the most demonic man on Earth's weakness is? If he has no soul, what's his weakness?"

Summarizing his role, McTavish says, "It definitely references moments from *Terminator* and *Predator* or any of those great 80s movies. But we also need to remember he isn't a robot, he is NOT the Terminator — he is a man who has suffered greatly.

"I took Clint Eastwood as a model, (who also inspired Garth Ennis), and re-watched all his Westerns," McTavish continues. "There's a power in silence, an eloquence, and something I learned long ago on stage was the value of stillness. I tried to bring those to the Saint from day one. His character is all about economy, both of movement and speech. The hardest part is trusting to the economy I just referred to, to sink into that stillness, to channel the feelings of profound grief and rage into a single expression, or word."

The actor reflects upon his dread, on-screen persona, to an extraordinary degree, forming conclusions that are insightful and rather touching. "The Saint is a great reader of history (maybe that's just me, but a lot of reading is done wearing those guns)," says McTavish.

"I always try and bring the spirit of his family into every scene. They are his purpose, his fuel. He is not a mindless killer. Whenever he pulls that trigger, he sees his daughter and wife, dead in front of him."

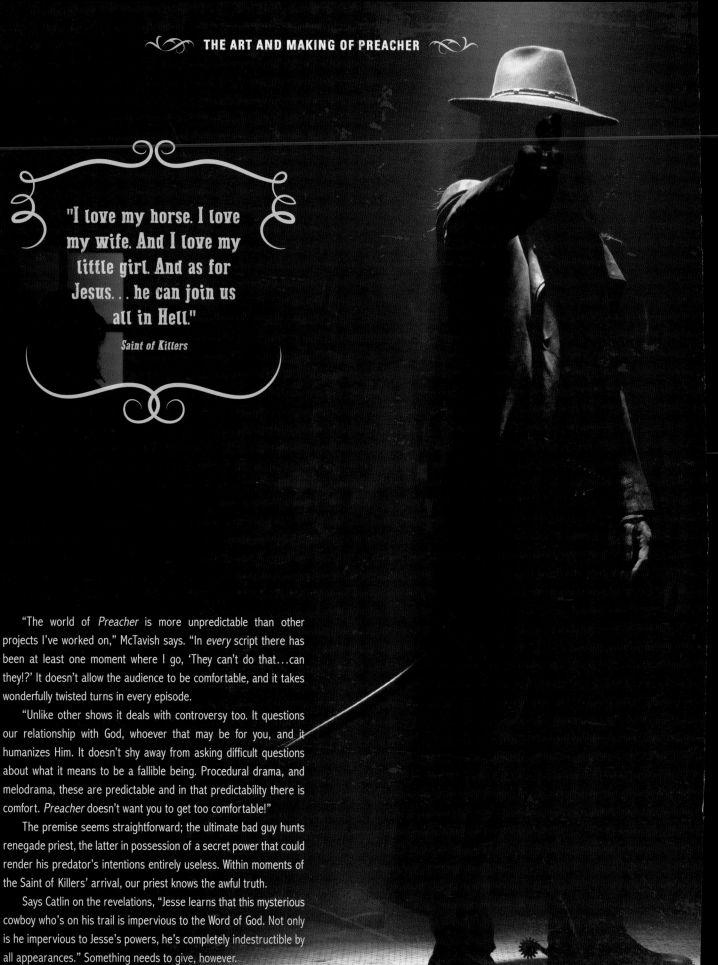

"I love my horse. I love my wife. And I love my little girl. And as for Jesus... he can join us all in Hell."

Saint of Killers

"The world of *Preacher* is more unpredictable than other projects I've worked on," McTavish says. "In *every* script there has been at least one moment where I go, 'They can't do that...can they!?' It doesn't allow the audience to be comfortable, and it takes wonderfully twisted turns in every episode.

"Unlike other shows it deals with controversy too. It questions our relationship with God, whoever that may be for you, and it humanizes Him. It doesn't shy away from asking difficult questions about what it means to be a fallible being. Procedural drama, and melodrama, these are predictable and in that predictability there is comfort. *Preacher* doesn't want you to get too comfortable!"

The premise seems straightforward; the ultimate bad guy hunts renegade priest, the latter in possession of a secret power that could render his predator's intentions entirely useless. Within moments of the Saint of Killers' arrival, our priest knows the awful truth.

Says Catlin on the revelations, "Jesse learns that this mysterious cowboy who's on his trail is impervious to the Word of God. Not only is he impervious to Jesse's powers, he's completely indestructible by all appearances." Something needs to give, however.

ABOVE AND BELOW: *This act of heroism from Cass to save Tulip proves, if any proof is needed, that he cares a great deal for her.*

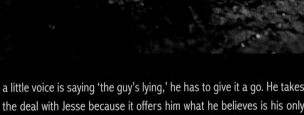

"Both the Saint and Jesse will never give up their chosen positions," explains McTavish. "Jesse is smart. The thing that governs him, more than anything, is his intellect."

Jesse hatches a plot, which requires winning the trust of the Saint of Killers — a seemingly impossible task. Yet Jesse is assured by the knowledge of what matters most to the Saint of Killers. "Jesse makes a huge leap of faith and offers him something in return for not hurting his friends," says Cooper. The Saint may well have declined. It's William that accepts.

Says McTavish, "Even though the Saint is by no means stupid, he has to try. He has to. Even though, probably at the back of his mind,

a little voice is saying 'the guy's lying,' he has to give it a go. He takes the deal with Jesse because it offers him what he believes is his only chance of getting back with his family."

In the few seconds after the Saint swallows the fragment of Jesse's soul, Jesse is in control.

"Jesse has the opportunity to allow him to go to Heaven, and chooses not to because he's vindictive and thinks that a man who sinned as much as the Saint doesn't deserve to go to Heaven," Goldberg specifies. The look on the Saint's face, according to McTavish, "Was more of a dawning realization on the part of the Saint, that he'd been tricked."

Observing the many strengths of the show, McTavish points to the production team dynamic as a defining factor. "Seth and Evan are huge fans of the books. Sam wasn't familiar with them before so he brings an objective balance to their fanboy enthusiasm. But the show needs both aspects to work. Seth and Evan are very fluid on set, open, and experimental. Sam, as well as being a bloody great writer, is able to bring a strong overview to the project, to know when to be faithful to the books, and when to remember that this is a TV show not a novel."

In the final act of Jesse and the Saint, we see the furious cowboy raised from the deep and released from his prison to seek the preacher one last time. A deal is struck between the Saint and agent Hoover of the Grail, and the next thing we know he is in Denis' apartment.

"We really like that the Saint doesn't barge into the place and start laying waste," Catlin says. "It's a different Saint. It's a cruel and more vengeful Saint. You're never going to win that fight. Whether [Jesse] has his weapons or not, the Saint is pretty much indestructible."

Goldberg is clearly happy with how the climactic battle plays. "The throw-down between Jesse, the Saint, as well as Tulip and Cassidy… everyone is going at everyone. The three of them are trying to take him out and they are hopelessly outmatched," Goldberg says. "It's like a David and Goliath story where David does not even have a rock."

Cooper is also impressed by the results, saying, "It really had to build to something special, and they put together a very exciting, complex but at the same amusing fight sequence."

ABOVE: This is the Saint back when he was plain William, a man who had moved beyond a dark past and built a life for himself with a loving wife and daughter. It's the love that William has for them that leads him to become the Saint of Killers.

After swatting aside both Cassidy and Tulip, at long last the Saint has Jesse in his clutches. He is ready to scalp Jesse, but is interrupted by Superintendent Mannering who calls him off. "It is a demonstration of power, I suppose," says Pip Torrens (Herr Starr). "It's showing that the Saint of Killers, who was always the one indestructible cosmic force, has now been relatively neutralized."

Indeed. Says Mannering as they leave: "You're lucky to have a man like Herr Starr looking out for you."

"One of the great strengths of Preacher is that all its principal characters are complicated," McTavish concludes. "No one is just evil, or good. They are human, and their relationships contain the complexity of any human relationship. We hurt those we love, and we sometimes understand the demons that drive us to cause that hurt."

BELOW: Jesse condemns the Saint to another type of Hell – trapped in an armoured truck at the bottom of a swamp.

"Talk quick, before I lose this bullet in your skull."

Saint of Killers to Jesse

SAINT OF KILLERS' HOMESTEAD

It hurts to look at this empty room, in knowledge of the memory it represents. The sense of a place is tangible throughout *Preacher*, thanks in no small part to superb cinematography, which with respect to the Saint of Killers' Homestead is down to John Grillo.

The Saint's homestead is a symbolic landmark, where we only see inside the room in which William stares hopelessly at the corpses of a beautiful family that he was unable to save. It is a simple cabin, with simple furnishings, now devoid of any happiness and tenderness that occupied the space between people who once lived there.

In 2017, Grillo was nominated for the American Society of Cinematographers Award for Outstanding Achievement in Cinematography in a Regular Series for Commercial Television.

RATWATER

Welcome to the Saint of Killers' worst memory: a Wild West town in 1881 that we snatch glimpses of in season 1 episodes 'See' and 'South Will Rise Again', before 'Finish the Song' reveals the whole wretched truth of his life. Director of photography John Grillo received his nomination for Outstanding Achievement in Cinematography by The American Society of Cinematographers for the Saint of Killers story. The scenes in their entirety are almost too harrowing to view a second time. In Hell, the Saint must relive the loss of his wife and only daughter in vivid, cruel reality for all eternity. The entire fifteen minute sequence can be watched on Grillo's website.

Acknowledging Grillo for his achievement in Regular Series for

Commercial Television, the ASC profiles how the Saint of Killers' sequence came to be: "In prep, Grillo studied the photogravures of Edward S. Curtis and the paintings of Andrew Wyeth for inspiration. For the Cowboy's flashback scenes, he wanted to imbue his digital material with as much texture as possible, using a combination of Panavision PVintage lenses, chocolate filters, and atmosphere on set to create the impression of an Old West photograph in motion. LiveGrain was used in post to add a pushed negative look to the footage."

Fans of the show were swift to notice how the hanging tree outside of town connected Annville to Ratwater, indicating that both

BELOW: *A dusty town in the desert complete with its own church.*

ABOVE: *The texture of the sets and photos gives a real sense of sun-bleached wood and desert-dry air.*

Godforsaken destinations reside in the same geographical location. It's where the Saint passes and we see Native Americans hanging from the branches during the flashback of 1881. It's also where we find Jesse and Cassidy exhuming the bodies of DeBlanc and Fiore to retrieve an angel hand before dumping the blanketed dead body of Mayor Miles Person and shoveling back the dirt in the darkness.

The "Towne of Ratwater" had its exteriors fabricated so that we can see the Saint of Killers arrive after riding day and night in hopes of retrieving medicine for his fading daughter. Though we join the Saint in the town apothecary for only a few moments, the interior is abundantly rigged, with specimen jars and all manner of wooden caddies and glass receptacles from which the scent of dried herbs might waft, disguising the stench of sweat.

It speaks to the detail lavished on this most memorable of locations that we observe the Saint through the windows of a schoolhouse, the children dashing about excitedly inside. Owing to how the Saint's story is fed to us throughout the three season 1 episodes we can only suspect that Ratwater's apparent normality is setting us up for something traumatic. The screeching soundtrack does an ample job of raising awareness of the imminent truth.

ABOVE: The detail of the sets and costume for the Ratwater section is incredible.

Cooley's Inn & Saloon is where the primary action takes place, with scenes of unspeakable depravity that the Saint chooses initially to ignore, focusing instead on the mission at hand. His fate is sealed, however, when he backtracks — medicine in possession — to save a family of pioneers from a similar ordeal to those he had witnessed the day before. We are taken into the backroom of the saloon where we find that the pioneer father is hawking scalps.

From the pioneer's abandoned wagon, where the Saint observes a dog lapping up clotted pools of blood, to the floorboards of Cooley's, which we hear drumming as a sack of heads drops at the Saint's heels, Ratwater creeps into our subconscious mind where it remains as a specter. We take on board the Saint's calculated response to the question of whether the West is paradise, indelible as one of the few times that we hear him speak.

"It ain't."

RIGHT: A lot of inspiration for the sets and the set dressing was taken from actual photographs from the period. The results are stunning.

ABOVE: It's worth poring over every inch of these photographs to get a full idea of the care and attention that went into the Ratwater scenes.

DENIS

RENOWNED FOR HIS depiction of serial killer Alexander Cambias in the long-running TV series *All My Children* (1991-2009), and with prior appearances in *The Hunt for Red October* (1990), *The Pillow Book* (1996), and *August Rush* (2007), Ronald Guttmann's performances have enhanced popular drama and blockbuster movies across four decades. With apparent ease, making the role all the more credible, Guttmann brings the required combination of frailty and obstinacy to his portrayal of Denis, Cassidy's heartbreakingly estranged, French-speaking eighty-year-old son.

Throughout *Preacher* we grow increasingly familiar with how its world starkly reflects in on itself through relationships between characters. The tension between Cassidy and Denis is a transcendent example, in what first appears to be a senior benefactor showing disinterest in his younger counterpart. It was the turning of tables — the younger guy being the father, while the older guy is in fact the disapproving son — that attracted Guttmann to the job.

RIGHT: *We never really get to know Denis. Does he want to reunited with his errant father, or is he just interested in being saved from death? We, and Cass, will never really know.*

ABOVE: *The relationship between youthful father Cass and aging son Denis throws up many questions — like how far would you go to save a dying relative?*

ABOVE: *We see Denis at his weakest — sick, dying, anchored to the toilet...*

ABOVE: *...until Cass relents and turns him into a virile, bloodthirsty monster.*

Joseph Gilgun takes this snapshot for the family album: "Denis' behavior is slightly changing. Cassidy doesn't know this man. All he's met is this sick, depressed version of what once was Denis. He's attempting to be a father. He's *trying*. And I think Denis is just happy to go along for the ride. I don't think Denis is there to rekindle a relationship with his father. I think Denis is just out for himself."

Denis signifies failure for Cassidy, and Cassidy suffers from private guilt at the way things turned out between them. Says Sam Catlin, "Denis, through his illness, gives Cassidy an opportunity to make up for all his past bad behavior in one fell swoop." However, Cassidy struggles with the implications.

Says Gilgun with a sorrowful look, "When Cassidy figures out that Denis wants to be bitten, wants to be a vampire, I think he's appalled. Cassidy knows that it's the wrong thing to do. The only reason that Cassidy bites Denis is to make himself feel better. He's selfish. There's a side to him that's just tremendously weak and really disappointing."

The decision to have Cassidy communicate with Denis via a translation device only adds to the pathos, and is a masterstroke.

DENIS' APARTMENT

The textured aesthetic of the show — which demands nothing less than intense scrutiny — is realized to its fullest potential in the home of eighty-year-old Denis. Also, Cassidy manages to play down his family association with such ease, we are left at the scriptwriters' mercy as to how their father and son relationship is revealed. Add to this, the point at which the Saint of Killers eventually tracks the team down and instantly turns upside down a seemingly quiet and cozy retreat. Mundane erupts into monstrous.

Of course, the most noteworthy transformation is that of Denis, from a frail and waning old man to a rejuvenated, no-respect, party animal. His pitiful deathbed becomes a teenager's den — although the music is, bizarrely, the stuff from his youth. In many ways, Denis' apartment reflects upon the contrast between everyday life for regular people, and the way that our group of misfits handle it: Tulip's incredibly unhealthy pancakes; Tulip and Featherstone playing videogames; conversations about favorite TV shows around the

ABOVE AND BELOW: *Like Ratwater, Denis' apartment looks like a fully functioning and lived-in space, and not a TV show set at all.*

breakfast table.

As the audience, we are always one step ahead, we have the view around the next corner, knowing that the friend down the hall is not who she seems, that the gang's most intimate moments are being observed, and that it'll take nothing less than 'divine' intervention to prevent the Saint of Killers from busting down the door after being led directly to them.

The climax of season 2 is hard-hitting because of how almost every relationship is tested to breaking point — either going up in flames or left bleeding on the floor.

ABOVE AND BELOW: The dim lighting and worn aesthetic creates a shabby space that is somehow quite cosy.

ABOVE AND BELOW: *Every piece of furniture, every stain, every bit of peeling paint, every carefully placed household item, they all add to the overall effect.*

GRAIL INDUSTRIES

Production Designer David Blass (*Secrets and Lies*, *Constantine*, *Pitch*) is the person we have to thank for such memorable locations as the Mumbai Sky Tower, Denis' apartment, Hell, and the venue we're now looking at: a division of Grail Industries. If you believe cleanliness is close to godliness, the aesthetic here is impeccably on point. It is precisely the place you'd expect to find Herr Starr: a commanding presence amid this pristine penthouse with a view.

Everything we are purposefully led to observe through our exposure to the Grail in season 2 is regimented to within a tiniest fraction of error. Indeed, an organization linked to Heaven may not waver in the slightest – from the recruitment process, which Herr Starr aces in cold, calculated fashion, through militarized operations

in the field, it is all so tremendously taut.

Events that transpire on Grail Industries property point to the fact that such regimentation is prone to exploitation from a character like Starr. Arguably, he cheats his way to the top, and then betrays the person who welcomes him there, claiming the topmost position via fair (you have to say) means wrought foul.

So much of how a scene looks influences our thoughts about events that we expect to play. Let's use the Featherstone nightclub crooning scene as an example. The classic portrayal, exactly as Featherstone requires Jesse to believe. With the Grail, we are caught entirely off-guard by Starr's callow behavior under the auspices of our Heavenly Father.

BELOW: *Was it the moment that Saltonstall relented and validated Starr's parking that showed his lack of ruthlessness? A lack that Starr exploited for his own gain?*

"Sometimes there is no substitution for hand-to-hand violence."

Saltonstall

ABOVE: One of the more extreme methods of vetting, which Starr seems to enjoy.

ABOVE: Herr Starr kills without compassion or rancour.

LARA & FJ HOOVER

JULIE ANN EMERY (*Better Call Saul*) and Malcolm Barrett (*Timeless*, *Better Off Ted*) nail every play in the *Preacher* book during season 2. As operatives of The Grail, led by Herr Starr's Samson Unit, the duo embodies the secrecy and menace laced with laughs and sass that defines the show. Both are ruthless, although Hoover fumbles while Featherstone takes point. *Preacher* is a

BELOW: Emery: "I slowly discovered that sometimes Featherstone does even smile… The trigger for that usually involves some sort of destruction…"

welcome opportunity for Emery, who says, "It is the thrill of my career to play such an extreme character. To play a character based in her own abilities and ambitions, rather than based in the fact that she is a woman."

Speaking of the potency of a collaboration between Seth Rogen, Evan Goldberg and Sam Catlin, Emery says, "*Preacher* is a genre mash-up that in theory shouldn't actually work, but on screen it does," she says. "Imagine that the guys behind *Sausage Party* got together with an Emmy Winning writer from *Breaking Bad*. It sounds insane, like it could never work. But THAT is *Preacher*. From singing, to dismantling a Glock mid-scene, to stunt work…who gets to do all of that while also taking such a deep dive into character and scene with such a prestige level cast? Honestly, I didn't think a job like this one existed until I walked onto our set. I am in heaven!"

On working with her on-screen partner, Emery describes, "Any scene with Malcolm Barrett (Hoover) is the easiest part of my job. The juxtaposition of our characters just works so easily." On Featherstone in isolation, Emery confides, "The hardest aspect of Featherstone for me was that the base of Featherstone herself is so rigid, so regimented and dark. It took some time to figure out where she lets her thoughts or feelings show through. The scenes that are the hardest to navigate are where Featherstone is unsure of herself: AKA anytime Herr Starr is in the room."

Barrett has his own take on the (un)holy trio's relationship: "The relationship between Herr Starr, Featherstone and Hoover is one of the sickest, most unhealthy love triangles I've ever seen and I love every moment of it. I love being the beta to Featherstone's alpha. I love seeing the humanity of Hoover versus the coarseness of Featherstone. We all vary on how far we're willing to go for the cause but we're seemingly all united in its purpose."

BELOW: *Emery: "Understanding all of the relationships is a deep dive. It really is the beating heart of the show."*

ABOVE: Emery: "There were crew members who introduced themselves to me three times because they didn't recognize me in a new character."

It's clear, owing to Barrett's performances, that Hoover is also conflicted and often scared by the tasks laid before him. He's not a killer. Indeed, he struggles to even slap Featherstone when pretending to be Rodney, the fictional abusive husband to Featherstone's undercover persona Jenny.

Says Barrett: "It's weird to play someone so inept yet useful. But that's part of what I love: the contradictions. I know Hoover's a 'bad guy', but he means well; that's kind of the secret to playing anyone 'evil.' They always have a virtuous motivation even if it's misguided, and that's why we're able to relate to them. And if you read Hoover's backstory from the comics, you get it. A villain is just a hero who's misunderstood."

Emery adds, "Featherstone is the only reason Hoover is still alive in this organization. She sees him as more of a little brother. Someone to protect. And part of that protection is kicking him in the ass until he gets his shit together. The fact that Hoover is in love with Featherstone, but is stuck in the friend/little brother zone makes the relationship all the more fantastic to play."

When offered the role of Hoover, Malcolm Barrett had no doubts:

"I love comic books and it's been a dream of mine to be in a live action version of a graphic novel. I was attracted to this show because of the style as well as the talent behind it – I've always been a fan of Seth and Evan's tone, and the humor and irreverence they bring to every project. Joining them in something so unforgiving in its approach and subject matter seemed right up my alley. After I binge-watched the first season, I read through as many of the comics as I could until I fell in love with Hoover."

And how does he feel now that he's survived one season of *Preacher*? "Filming *Preacher* has been a wholly unique experience if for no other reason than the content and the boundaries we push. I faithfully follow a crypto-fascist leader with rape fantasy tendencies, my partner is a zealot and a killer, and I somehow consider myself sweet while wholly participating in all sorts of debauchery."

Featherstone could be read as selfless *or* selfish, although the evidence suggests the latter when she is seen trying to impress her commander. "Herr Starr is a relationship that doesn't work in Featherstone's life," explains Emery. "She has no idea how to find a way in. She is such an expert manipulator. It is a big part of

ABOVE: Emery: "I've never been on a project where the comedy and the drama were both stretched so far and work on such a high level."

what makes her brilliant at her job. But she cannot understand or manipulate Starr. And she can't catch a break with him no matter what she does. He can't even remember her name! Every time he calls her the wrong name, a little piece of Featherstone dies."

Regarding her scenes as Featherstone masquerading as plain-Jane Jenny, Emery walks us through the premise: "Really (season 2, episode 10 'Dirty Little Secrets') is about creating a deeper relationship with Tulip and using that to manipulate her into leaving Jesse. Featherstone is not in a real relationship with Tulip, she is using her intense research to push Tulip in the direction she needs her to go. Tulip and Featherstone are playing out a girlfriends relationship that neither of them is capable of having in their normal life. They are both playing at something they don't fully understand."

It also shows how Tulip is seeking a connection with another human being, even if she has doubts. This introduces tension that is only dissipated after Featherstone pulls the trigger that drops Tulip like a stone. It's a moment that takes your breath away.

"Once Tulip understands what's happening in that room, Featherstone thinks in a straight line, and Tulip is just in the way," Emery explains. "There's something flat and dark about Featherstone that allows her to do things that a normal human being would be mortified by."

Emery goes further to explore her character's motivations: "Featherstone is a true believer. If she has to blow up the world in order to save it, she is ready, willing, and eager. This is what makes her so dangerous. It is also why understanding a character like her in the world we live in is important. Zealotry is a dangerous thing."

HERR STARR

NEAT AS A pin, and driven as the nails that pierced his (original) Messiah, Herr Starr makes the most dramatic of about turns during season 2. With seconds to spare, Starr calls off an air strike that would evaporate Jesse Custer, a sitting duck within his New Orleans hideout. But far from betraying his cause, Starr has discovered a more efficient way forward.

"Herr Starr is clearly not the regular kind of conscript. I prefer to think of him as just very linear," says Pip Torrens, cracking the slightest of smiles. The actor's dapper conduct and elegant diction has served him well in roles such as the Netherfield butler in *Pride & Prejudice* (2005) and the First Order's Colonel Kaplan in *Star Wars: The Force Awakens* (2015). His character Cary Warleggan in *Poldark* (2015) is cold and ruthless — qualities Herr Starr has in spades.

As Evan Goldberg outlines, "Herr Starr is an agent of the Grail — the largest and oldest secret society that runs the entire world.

The Samson Unit is a special unit dedicated to finding false messiahs, besides the Grail's own Messiah, and killing them."

"We see him go through almost a supervillain training camp," explains Seth Rogen, "where evil people are eliminated one by one, leaving only the Most Evil. He's auditioning to be the second in charge of Samson Unit. He then kills the guy who's in charge of it, and then becomes the head of Samson Unit." Confirms Torrens, "[Starr] immediately makes his presence felt."

However, Starr is no puppet in his servitude. Regarding his holy purpose, says Rogen, "Herr Starr doesn't believe or care about any of that, and seems more to think they're just a means for him to become incredibly powerful."

Even while marshalling the troops and ensuring missions are going to plan, Starr's best people must remain attentive, in case of diversions. Starr may find inspiration for the next best course of action under the most bizarre of circumstances — such as indulging in a rape fantasy, albeit not exactly what he originally had in mind.

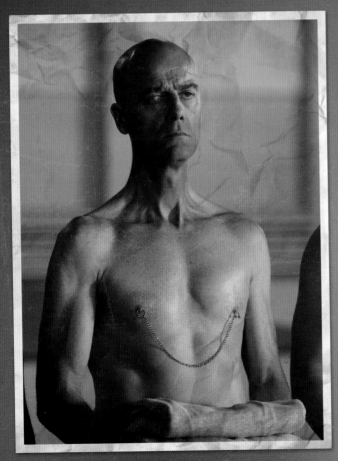

ABOVE: Torrens: "My fellow cast are so great in their roles that being vile to them is surprisingly easy."

ABOVE: Torrens: "Playing an extreme character like Starr is extremely therapeutic, as long as I leave him at work."

Says Torrens, "Starr's sex life is an ongoing experiment. For him to be humiliated can lead to moments of clarity." Rather than tearing Genesis and Custer asunder, Starr brings the full package on board. "Starr sees in Jesse something that he feels is a brand, that can continue and take them both to a completely different level of world domination," states Torrens.

"He's trying to create a Messiah that he can control," details Rogen. "But he's also trying to create a Messiah who believes he's the Messiah. So, he's got to convince Jesse that he indeed should run the universe."

Jesse's inaugural field mission brings season 2 to a fine conclusion. "Certainly, it's very odd to see Starr and Jesse in a classroom of adorable kiddies. It's almost like a Bible study group, which is then interrupted by a battle with these Armenians, four of the most terrifying guys you'll ever see," Torrens summarizes with a hint of mirth. "It's very funny because clearly Starr's set this up. I think he's seeing how it goes, you know. He's enjoying himself. We're off to this whole new, real world section that we haven't really addressed before."

BELOW AND BELOW RIGHT: Herr Starr enjoys various hobbies, such as making strange requests of his dates and...esoteric movies.

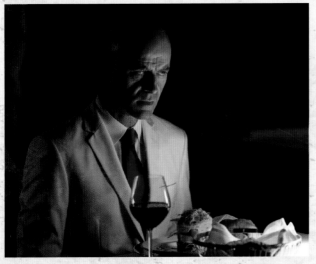

HELL

This stark holding facility is oddly neutral in terms of emotional impact. It's the people trapped there who concern us the most. People like Adolf Hitler, although only on one occasion does the world's most haunting man exhibit the kind of behavior we'd expect. We suspect, however, that all is not what it seems, and in particular the physical manifestation of Superintendent Mannering — a matronly high-ranking guard with a tendency to speak in guttural tones.

In *Preacher*, Hell is the worst cinema multiplex experience ever devised. Damnation is the repeated, private viewing of your life's worst memory, in wholly convincing virtual reality. The foyer equivalent is the common room where inmates gather between screenings, to beat each other up over minor transgressions, and never show the slightest consideration toward another soul. Misbehave, and you get dumped into a literal Hell-hole, where misery and torment are considerably amplified. It's unsettling because everything seems otherwise normal, even Hitler. Through Eugene 'Arseface' Root, we question in all solemnity just what, in Hell, is going on. That a guy named Tyler seems the nastiest piece of work around doesn't seem right at all. But you start to notice that the production design has a hint of the distant past about it, that the architecture is the stuff of Ancient Astronaut theory, or just as wild.

Hell's clean lines, although shabby by comparison, appear to complement the immaculate corridors of a Grail Industries skyscraper. Not a coincidence, since both concepts are the work of production designer David Blass.

BELOW AND FAR RIGHT: *Hell is a nightmare of Brutalist architecture, hard angles, curved screens and disorientating lighting.*

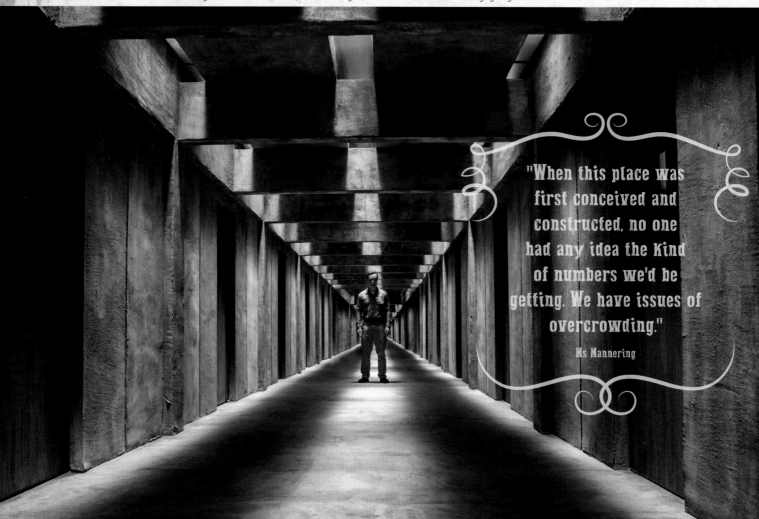

"When this place was first conceived and constructed, no one had any idea the kind of numbers we'd be getting. We have issues of overcrowding."

Ms Mannering

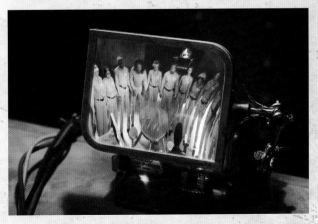

ABOVE, BELOW AND FAR RIGHT: The hell of Hell is living out your worst memory over and over again in a stark. cold cell.

"You think your worst
memory's bad? You think
that's torture? We can
make it worse."

HITLER

YOU'RE IN HELL. Who do you see?

Seth Rogen: "We're just going to do the thing everyone is thinking. If you're going to go to Hell, you should probably have Hitler around."

The 'Eugene meets Hitler' vignettes are irresistible viewing in *Preacher*; our doleful Texan boy served as cute and cuddly prey to the deadliest of vipers. For such a premise to work, however, the notorious dictator needed to show a vulnerable, redeemable side. Historically, the very suggestion has often looked like career suicide for Rogen.

"We're known for humanizing horrible dictators," laughs Rogen. "That's kind of our thing. I've been fired from three TV shows for pitching Hitler as a main character."

Evan Goldberg adds that, "Most of the time we watch television, we're constantly asking why Hitler isn't a character in the given show. And we said, we're not going to be like the rest — we're going to make the right choice and make it now."

Noah Taylor, who has appeared in *Shine* (1996), *Vanilla Sky*

ABOVE: *There's a moral ambiguity to the Hitler we meet in Preacher — which is strange when we consider what he did, and what he represents. Does he really seek forgiveness? Or is he just playing Eugene in order to escape the Hell he so richly deserves?*

(2001), *Game of Thrones* (2013-2014) and *Paddington 2* (2017), is eminently adaptable as a performer, and tricky (if not impossible) to pigeonhole. As a passionate, softly spoken Adolf Hitler, he is unnerving.

Says Taylor of his thoughts approaching the provocative role: "Any dictator or strong man, they're usually a weak person backed by a lot of people. Once you take away the mystique of that sort of person, you recognize them as weak."

"To Eugene," explains Goldberg, "Hitler's presenting himself as a man who fully realizes that what he did was wrong. He's quite regretful and is just trying to be a good guy."

In Hell, all captives are subjected to repeated run-throughs of their life's worst memory. Hitler's torment is not what anyone expected. It's so…lame. The rationalization he shares with Eugene is that this was "the last day that I was good." Maybe, Eugene begins to think, Hitler isn't inherently evil?

Taylor comments that, "Hitler's most troubling memory is a very, very trivial one. But who's to say what sets someone off? He has a depraved lack of introspection, if that's the case. It just serves to make him an even more pathetic character."

Goldberg breaks down the scenario…

"Hitler's on a date with a beautiful girl, showing her his art and ordering plum cake. It turns into a nightmare for him, where a homosexual, a communist, a Jew, and the girl he's dating, all summarily make him feel terrible. He does not receive the plum cake he wants. This shatters his confidence and fills him with such hatred that he becomes Hitler."

BELOW: *A strange alliance grows between these opposites: one man who deserves his eternity of punishment, and another who does not.*

ABOVE: Hitler's worst memory is of a disastrous date in an up-market German restaurant, where he is humiliated over and over again.

ABOVE AND BELOW: In Hell Hitler proves not to be the Ubermensch he claimed to be. He is a weakling, preyed upon and beaten by his fellow inmates.

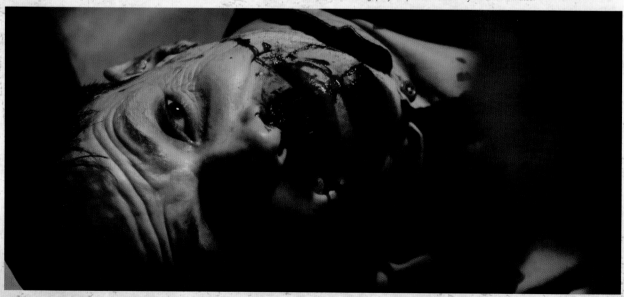

"You're Hitler. You started World War 2. You killed millions of people."

Eugene to Hitler

MS MANNERING

KNOWING THAT THE gifted character actress Amy Hill is universally loved and respected by both fans and colleagues, it makes you wonder how such a wonderful person winds up running actual Hell. This is what Hill has to say about playing an unfathomable character like Mannering: "I'm naturally soft, gentle and very sweet (really!), so being so hard-edged was difficult. The directors helped keep me honestly evil, which was hard for me to gauge."

She goes on: "I was interested in the challenge of being in charge of "Hell". When would I have an opportunity to portray someone so evil, who enjoyed torturing her inmates with such pleasure? I hoped to be able to create a fully realized character who had a backstory, and I think I was given the opportunity to do that. It was a joy to see what evolved."

Hill, who has performed recurring roles for popular TV dramas, while appearing in countless Hollywood movies and voicing all manner of animated characters, has also made a success from stand-up in recent years. Given her humor and tendency to perform a very neighborly, motherly role, it's therefore striking to see Hill as

ABOVE: *Ms Mannering has a lot of responsibility — and she has to answer to you-know-who if things go wrong.*
BELOW: *A Spartan office of concrete and stone, designed to intimidate.*

> "This is Hell.
> Act accordingly."
>
> Ms Mannering

stony-faced Superintendent Mannering. "I think," she says, "with age, my face has evolved into what is termed 'resting bitch' because I seem to get more parts like this."

It is apt, however, that Mannering could be seen as a parental figure, albeit one who has seen more than enough and has drawn a line that is absolute. Bizarre, guttural sounds that occasionally distort her voice are a design choice, clueing audiences in to the demonic truth. She suggests that there were several aspects of the production that helped her inhabit her role:

"The location fed a lot of the nuances for me. Even though I was in Hell, the depth of the city, in its history, challenges and supernatural nature, kept me in a sort of otherworldly space. It was a great experience and the nature of the project was refreshing. My background in theater, improvisation and performance art was helpful. [The production] was a very relaxed, safe place to explore and create. For creative people, it's important to be able to feel that way. The whole cast and crew was generous, kind, supportive and fun."

That Mannering can softly command the Saint of Killers without issue is testament to the warden's individual strength, and position within Satan's hierarchy. Yet Hill maintains that there's a surprising hidden side to Ms Mannering. Let's give her the last word: "All my characters are in search of love. I believe Mannering is, too. She just has no idea how to do it and is severely misguided. Severely misguided."

SAINT VERSUS COPS

Way to open a TV show. This spectacular action scene catapults the viewer into the crazy, violent and humorous world of *Preacher*. Jesse, Tulip and Cassidy have been pulled over by the cops. Jesse, armed with Genesis, thinks he's got things under control. Until the Cowboy from Hell appears...

Season Two, Episode One: Directed by Seth Rogen and Evan Goldberg. Storyboards by Robin Richesson

1A

EXT SIDE of HWY, DAY
Cops have hauled Jesse and Tulip out of the Chevelle, and
    SLAM them onto hood
Tulip: *"There's gonna be a plan here, right?"*

1B

CONT
CAM move around to profile on Jesse
"Sure" (not really)

1C

CONT
CAM move up to GRUFF SGT
"Alright freak, drop the grass and the umbrella!"

1D

CONT
CAM PAN to Cassidy, emerging from Chevelle, with a joint
    and his umbrella
OS Gruff SGT: *"RIGHT NOW!"*

1E

CONT
Cassidy flicks joint away, backing up
*"But guys, I really need this umbrella or I burst into
    flames..."*

2

Alternate Coverage, rising up with crane
"...Lemme just..."
Cassidy is reaching into a pocket
Officers: *"HANDS! HANDS! HANDS!"*

3

(in same shot as previous page, Med on Cassidy)
"…Lemme just…"

4

CUT TO Officers, Guns drawn
"HANDS! HANDS! HANDS!"

5A

CUT BACK TO Cassidy, Med
"Relax! I'm just gettin'…"
Officers rush him and tackle,

5B

CONT
They pull him out of frame…

5C

CONT
HOLD on EMPTY FRAME
Highway stretches into distance (nothing there…?)

6A

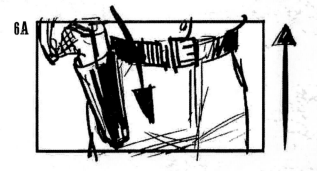

CUT TO
Gun being holstered,
CAM UP

6B

CONT
To Gruff SGT.
He looks, as Baby Faced Officer walks Cassidy over towards him
    carrying the umbrella to shade Cassidy (in cuffs)

6C

CONT
CAM follow Gruff SGT as he steps towards them,
GS: *"What the hell are you doing?"*

6D

CONT
CAM around to a THREE SHOT
BF: *"He said he'd catch fire."*

6E

CONT
GS: *"Idiot."*

6F

CONT
Gruff SGT bats umbrella away,
Cassidy's arm starts to smoke…

6G

CONT
Cassidy runs to a Patrol CAR
"AHHHHH!"

6H

CONT
CAM PAN him into back seat

7A

CUT TO
Over Gruff SGT. On Baby Face
"Guess he was telling the truth…" etc

7B

CONT
Gruff SGT turns to look towards car, MEAN smile breaks across
his face…

8A

CUT TO, Cassidy POV, GS comes to window
*"Come on out here, boy, just wanna ask you a few
questions, out here in the sunshine."*

8B

CONT
He reaches in towards Cassidy

9

CUT TO Reverse on Cassidy, recoiling
O.S. Jesse: *"Stop!"*
(Gruff SGT. hand freezes!)

10

CUT TO
Jesse, Tulip nearby
(WoG) *"HOLSTER YOUR GUNS."*

11

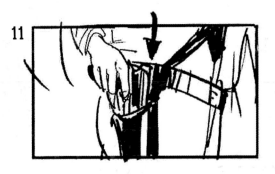

CUT TO SERIES of quick beats, Officers holster their guns

12

CUT TO

13

"What the...?!"

14A

CUT TO Behind Jesse,
"SHUT YOUR MOUTH."
"STEP OVER THERE."

14B

CONT
They all edge over into a cluster

15

CUT TO CU Jesse
"YOU"
(he nods at a heavy set cop)

16

CUT TO Worried React from Heavy Set Cop

17

CUT BACK to Jesse
"GAS UP OUR CAR."

18A

CUT BACK to Heavy Set Cop
CAM follow him to vehicle,

18B

CONT
He moves box of FLARES aside, as he gets out a jerry can
    of GAS

19A

CUT TO Over Tulip,
As she watches this unfold,

19B

CONT
She turns to look over at Jesse
"Nice plan."
"Let's get Cassidy and go."

19C

CONT
CAM moves off her onto Jesse (he isn't listening)
"YOU, MACE YOUR BALLS."
(to Gruff SGT.)

20

Wide on Officers, Gruff SGT. takes out Mace, unzips his fly and sprays into his pants

21

(INSERT React CU on Gruff SGT?
This could also be coverage for when Jesse tells him to shut his mouth)

22

CUT TO TIGHT CU Jesse,
"YOU TWO. HOLD HANDS."

23A

CUT TO TWO SHOT,
Officers obey

23B

CONT

24

CUT BACK TO Tight CU Jesse
"YOU. RECITE THE STATE SONG."

25

CUT TO Baby Face,
He starts to recite (sing?):
"Texas, our Texas! All hail the mighty state…"

26A

CUT TO Tulip, Med, pushing in, she is fidgeting, not liking this

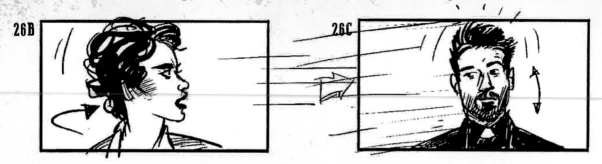

26B

End push on CU, she snaps her head on line: JESSE.
WHIP PAN to

26C

Jesse,
He snaps out of it,
Tulip O.S. *"Get Cassidy."*
He nods, exits frame

26D

CAM TRACK back with Jesse, he walks towards SUV where
Cassidy is,

26E

CONT
Cop with gas passes him, a distant crack is heard

26F

CONT
then suddenly the Cop's guts spray out his side, he falls

27

CUT TO Reverse on Jesse, he hears the thud, looks in
confusion

28A

CUT TO Jesse POV of DEAD COP, guts on pavement, gas can on
the ground,
CAM move off body to

28B

CONT
CAM onto Tulip, standing near Chevelle, shrugs, like WTF

29

CUT BACK to Jesse,
he looks over to group of COPS, they are all agitated,
    looking around (they can't speak, except for Baby Face
    still recites song)

30

CUT TO POV of Cops,

31

CUT BACK TO Jesse, as he looks around,

32A

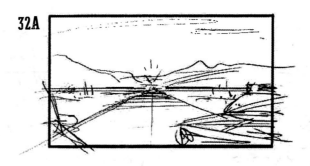

CUT TO his POV
we see a tiny glint, in the distance down the highway

31

CUT BACK TO Jesse, push in as he says:
"Everyone down!"

32A

CUT TO Steady CAM shot, on Cops, chaos, they all run
    for cover, one (baby face?) runs past CAM, and CAM
    follows with him

32B

CONT Steady CAM, as it picks up Gruff SGT.
He is running towards Chevelle,

32c

CONT
Coming closer to CAM,

32D

CONT
BLAM! his head is blown off
CAM follow him to the ground,

32E

He lands not far from Tulip, CAM onto her, she looks to
Jesse,

33A

CUT TO Jesse
CAM moves around Jesse as he surveys the situation,
some COPS are crouched by the Patrol Cars, they
beckon the other cops to join them and defend,

33B

CONT around to CU Jesse
"SMOKE"

34A

CUT Back to Tulip, she dashes over towards Jesse, (and
the car with flares)
CAM is leading Tulip

34B

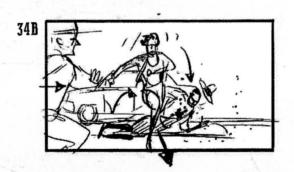

CONT Coverage of CAM leading Tulip, same action of Cops
running across frame towards their buddies, they get
hit and fall, she dodges and leaps over their bodies

ALT

ALTERNATE COVERAGE,
CAM tracks with her, as COPS run past her towards the
beckoning Cops, a few are hit, and go down, she dodges and
leaps over their bodies.

34C

CONT

34D

CONT as Tulip runs past Jesse, and he heads for "gas" car,

34E

CONT CAM pulls back from PAN to see Tulip grab a flare from trunk, as Jesse jumps in patrol car,

35

CUT TO INSERT
Tulips hits flare on her thigh to light it

36

CUT TO INT Patrol Car, Jesse, grabs rifle, pulls up parking brake, jams rifle onto gas pedal,

37

INSERT on Rifle BUTT on GAS PEDAL,

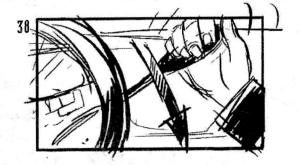

38

INSERT as Jesse puts SHIFTER into DRIVE

39A

CUT TO Tulip, has lit a flare,

39B

CONT
she brings it onto rear tire, which is spinning, it starts
    smoking

39C

CUT to Wide shot, Tulip and Jesse dash towards CAM, as
    CAM HINGES around them,

39D

CONT
PAN with them

39E

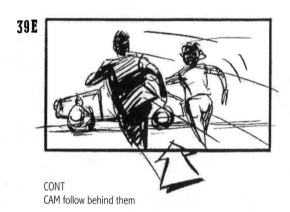

CONT
CAM follow behind them

40A

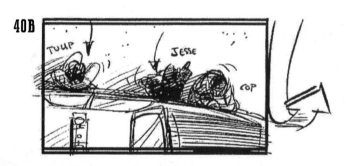

CUT TO in front of Tulip and Jesse running to CAM
CAM PULLS BACK AND UP

40B

CONT
Into OVERHEAD SHOT
on Tulip and Jesse arriving at one of the "frontline" Patrol
    Cars, joining one of the Cops crouched down there

40C

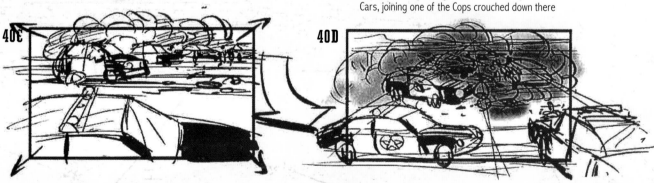

CONT
CAM slides over Patrol Car, Angle on the scene,

40D

CONT
to WIDE on Scene, SMOKE is filling the area,

41

CUT TO Shots of Stuff and people getting destroyed, on
Tulip, part of car above her is blown away...

41A

CUT TO
COP raising gun,

41B

CONT
his forearm gets blown off, gun goes flying,

42A

CUT TO
DRIVER'S Window is BLOWN OUT of SUV

42B

CONT
CAM PUSH IN to see CASSIDY, handcuffed, in the backseat,
freaked out, he ducks down

43A

CUT TO angle on Cassidy, his back against the door, as he
crouches on the floor

43B

CONT
"BLAM!" bullet rips a hole in the roof of the car, light streams
onto Cassidy, he starts to sizzle

44

CUT TO his POV to the tear in the roof

45A

CUT TO new overhead angle, Cassidy crawls over out of
the light

45B

CONT
Then, BLAM!, another hole is blown in the roof, light floods
in, he quickly tries to crawl into the shade again,

46

CUT to Cassidy POV of LARGE HOLE in roof

45C

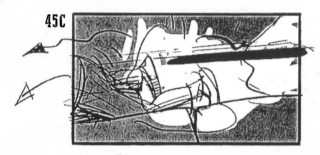

CONT
More shots are heard, and he panics and scoots out of
the car entirely…

47A

Cut to Raking Angle on Car, as Cassidy flops out onto
ground

47B

CONT
And quickly slides under the car to shade

48A

CUT TO WIDE on Patrol cars at "frontline", Cop, Jesse and Tulip
are crouched together,
CAM PUSH IN

48B

TO TIGHT THREE SHOT,

48C

CONT
Cop barely raises up to peek over the hood of the car,
    Jesse warns him,
SFX BLAM!

48D

CONT
Cop slumps back into frame, ¾ of his head missing

49A

CUT TO Jesse POV ish, past bloody head, SNAP ZOOM to
    Cops at adjacent car reacting

49B

CONT
They vigorously return fire

50A

CUT to Angle on Dead Cop, as he falls out of frame,
    revealing Jesse and Tulip stacked, CAM PUSH IN

50B

CONT
Tulip: What kind of gun is that?
Jesse looks to her

51A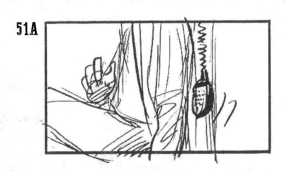

CUT TO Tight Shot on dangling P.A. handset,
He grabs it

51B

CONT
CAM follow it up to his face, as he prepares to speak in
    the WoG,

52A

CUT TO Wider TWO SHOT OF Jesse and Tulip,
CAM PUSH IN

52B

CONT PUSH IN,
As "BOOM" the car door between them is BLOWN OFF,
    taking handset cord with it

52C

CONT
Gaping HOLE (or entire door is GONE?)
Severed cord dangles
Jesse tosses Handset

53A

POV on Adjacent Car,
Fast Push in on their reaction

53B

CONT
They are panicking now, firing like crazy

53C

CONT
One by one they are successively picked off,

53D

CONT

54A

CUT TO Wider on Jesse and Tulip, pushing in

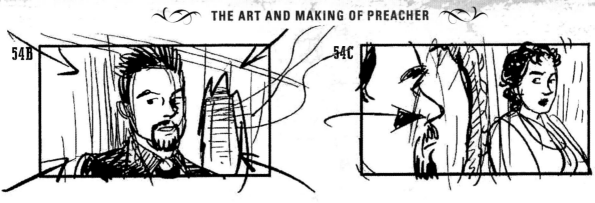

54B

CONT
PUSH IN ON Jesse,
"Time to go."

54C

CONT
Push past Jesse and he turns to look at Tulip
"I'm not leaving my car."

55A

CUT to TWO SHOT
Jesse: *"Where's Cassidy?"*

56A

CUT TO POV of Umbrella, lying in the road, slight PAN to
SUV (a dark shape is seen under the car?)

54D

CUT BACK TO Jesse and Tulip
T: *"I'm not leaving my car, Jesse."*
J: *"Then you better siphon some gas."*
T: *"Siphon? With what?"*

56B

CUT OFF Jesse's look to see pile of steaming guts on
pavement.

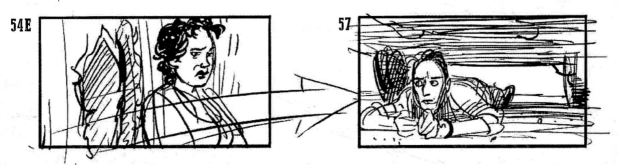

54E

CUT BACK TO Jesse and Tulip,
Jesse wipes frame and exits,
Tulip looks disgusted as she contemplates the thought.

57

Cassidy under SUV

55A

CUT TO his POV
Feet of Cop run by

55B

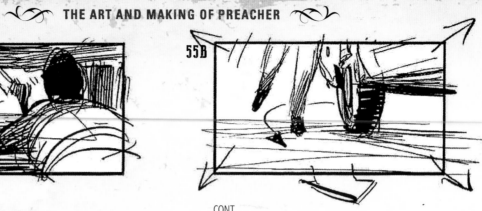

CONT
CAM Track across to see feet coming around to driver's
side of car PULLING OUT

55C

CONT
COP is holding the severed hand of his "partner" as he
jumps in the driver's seat,
CAM COMES Around,

55D

CONT ONTO COP
As he throws the car into...

55E

CONT
"BLAM"
his head explodes from another shot,

56

CUT TO INSERT of Shifter panel, splattered with blood, he
only made it to NEUTRAL

55F

CUT BACK TO COP, he slumps onto steering wheel (or maybe
this should be "DRIVE", with no foot on gas, car just idles
forward?)

56A

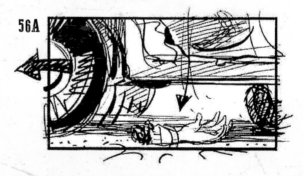

COVERAGE of "partner" hand, dropping to ground
as SUV starts to roll forward

56B

CONT
To pick up Cassidy, as he shimmies forward

57

CUT TO WIDE on CAR Rolling
we see Cassidy losing ground beneath the car.

58A

CUT TO Under SUV onto Cassidy, he glances back noticing
that he is in danger of exposure soon

59

CUT TO his POV, his feet are starting to stick out beyond
the SUV into the LIGHT

60

CUT TO Cassidy react (REV ANGLE)

61

CUT TO OVERHEAD Angle over rear bumper, Cassidy's feet
and ankles start to appear
He is still trying to scramble forward

58B

CUT BACK TO Cassidy, he is thrilled to see...

62
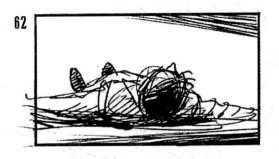

CUT TO HIS POV, a DEAD COP just to the side of the car as
it rolls along

63A

CUT TO Overhead, SUV, we see Cassidy's arm shoot out
and clutch the body and drag it partially

63B

CONT
under the SUV

64A

CUT TO ANGLE on the Head of the DEAD COP, as it
becomes a BLOCK to stop the SUV from rolling

64B

CONT TO CASSIDY, relieved,

64C

CONT
Until he sees

65

CUT TO POV of spilled GAS CAN, Gas is spreading across
pavement towards a lit JOINT that he tossed earlier
SNAP ZOOM onto JOINT,
(Background: Tulip runs past, grabbing a length of "GUTS")

24D

CUT BACK TO CASSIDY,
he inches over and tries to blow it out,

65

CUT TO TIGHT on JOINT, the blowing just makes it glow
stronger
off screen we hear the crackle and crunch

64E

CUT TO CASSIDY as he looks to see

64F

CUT TO ANGLE on the DEAD COP'S HEAD, getting crushed
at last by the SUV TIRE

66

CUT TO OVERHEAD Angle, SUV has started rolling again,
Cassidy's legs are starting to emerge from under the
vehicle

67A

CUT BACK TO Cassidy, he is giving up, resigned...

67B

CONT
The SUV clears him, and his head is down, eyes tight shut,
waiting for the LIGHT, but,

67C

CONT
he's somehow still shaded!
he looks around

67D

CONT
then UP,
to see

68

CUT TO Cassidy POV of Jesse, standing next to him holding
the umbrella over him

69A

CUT TO
Cassidy and Jesse RUN towards Chevelle, as SUV bursts
    into FLAMES
(GAS hits JOINT)

69B

CONT
CAM IS ACTUALLY PULLING BACK through the Chevelle, as
    they hop into the backseat,

69C

CONT
Followed by TULIP, jumping into the driver's seat

69D

CONT
CAM PAN over to her as she revs engine, and takes off

69E

CONT
Chevelle wipes frame
Speeds away, exiting frame

70

CUT TO REAR Windshield of Chevelle, Jesse twists round
    to see

71A

CUT TO JESSE POV ish angle on Patrol Car, a Cop runs to get
    into it,

71B

CONT
CAR screeches around, heading out towards the Chevelle

71C

CONT
BLAM! Bullet exploded through the COP and windshield,
blasting glass and blood

72

CUT BACK TO TIGHTER on Jesse as he watches
(a push in on shot 59, or a new tight shot)

73

CUT TO Jesse (moving) POV of a figure (Saint of Killers)
emerging out of the Fire, Smoke and Chaos

74

CUT BACK TO TIGHT CU of Jesse, as the reflection of the
fire plays on the window.

ENTER THE SAINT

This short sequence neatly adds the second bookend to the end of the first episode, with our trio once again being menaced by the unstoppable Saint of Killers, proving that no matter where they hide, or how fast a car they have, he'll find them eventually. It ends the episode on a killer cliffhanger.

Season Two, Episode One: Directed by Seth Rogen and Evan Goldberg. Storyboards by Robin Richesson

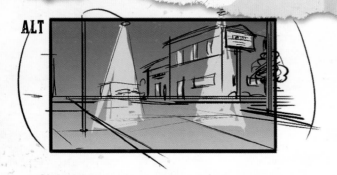

ALT

Coverage of Motel EXT

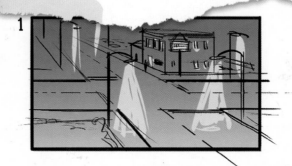

1

START
High and Wide on Motel a figure (Jesse) walks out onto sidewalk, smoking a cigarette

2A

CUT to behind Jesse,
CAM Around him

2B

CONT
onto Jesse as he finishes his cigarette,
tosses it,

2C

CONT
he turns to go back inside...

2D

CONT
Jesse sees...
CAM PUSH IN

3A

CUT TO Jesse POV
in the distance, a figure approaches
(The FIGURE goes in and OUT of street lamp light)

3B

CONT
he's gone,

3C

CONT
then appears again under the next light, a bit closer now

3D

CONT
disappears in darkness again

3E

CONT
Appears again, closer,
he is coming for sure

4

CUT TO LOW ANGLE on JESSE
head to toe

5A

CUT TO TIGHT CU Jesse,
he uses WoG
"STOP"

6

CUT TO POV,
Street is DARK and EMPTY
(did he stop?)

5B

CUT BACK TO CU JESSE
He takes a step Forward to CAM,
looking intently for anything

6B

CUT TO Jesse POV,
Dark street...

6C

CONT then before our eyes the FIGURE Emerges back into
   the light,
He's still COMING

7A

CUT TO MED CU on Saint of Killers,
CAM PUSH IN a bit,
AS HE SIMULTANEOUSLY

7B

CONT
RAISES his gun

8

CUT BACK to JESSE, head to toe,
FAST PUSH INTO CU
END SEQUENCE

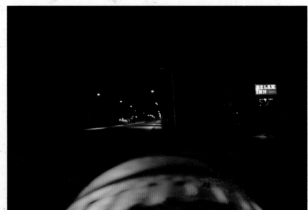

SAINT VS GUN CLUB

The second episode picks up right where the first ended: a dark street, a motel, and Jesse exposed to the Saint's lethal guns. Jesse already knows that Genesis does not work. He's about to find out that not even the combined firepower of the Greater Association of Gun Aficionados will be able to help.

Season Two, Episode One: Directed by Seth Rogen and Evan Goldberg. Storyboards by Robin Richesson

START on BOOTS,
Coming at us, CAM tracking back
Thunderous footfalls, BOOM...

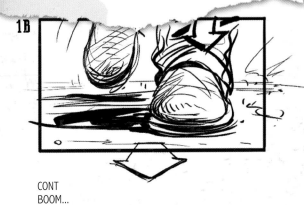

CONT
BOOM...

CONT
(YELLOW LIGHT is reflected on the boots)
BOOM...

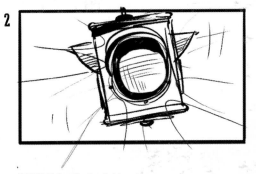

CUT TO Yellow Caution light, swings on a wire
FLASHING in time with the sound of footfalls

CUT TO
ECU on Mouth as cheeseburger comes in
CAM PULL OUT

CONT
PULL OUT TO show Heavy set guy in a van, eating fast food

4A

CUT TO
WHEEL in motion on a SEMI TRUCK
CAM goes up

4B

CONT
Woman driver, rubs her very tired eyes,

4C

CONT
she struggles not to nod off

5A

CUT TO
SIGN of MOTEL
CAM TILT DOWN

5B

CONT
CAM Find JESSE,
standing on the street below

6A

CUT TO Med on Jesse
CAM around

6B

CONT
Over Jesse,
Saint of Killers in distance

7

CUT TO
MED on Saint,
he raises his gun

8A

CUT TO INSIDE Barrel of GUN, worn and scarred
(BULLET POV)
JESSE is in the center of the shot

8B

CONT
Bullet enters frame as the shot leaves the barrel, zooms
towards Jesse

8C

CONT

8D

CONT
VAN wipes frame,

8E

CONT
as Bullet speeds forward they converge,

9A

CUT TO
Frontal shot outside VAN, Driver is hit, head explodes,
splatters on windshield, Driver Swerves

9B

CONT
VAN wipes out of frame

10A

CUT TO Behind VAN, it swerves over
CAM SLIDES Across as VAN heads towards other side of
the road

10B

CONT
Behind VAN, it swerves over

10C

CONT
CAM PAN with VAN as it hits pole of SIGN

11A

CUT TO Angle on SIGN as it falls

11B

CONT
CAM Tilts and follows it down to street
BAM!

11C

CONT
CAM moves up to reveal SEMI TRUCK heading for the
intersection

12

CUT TO
Driver, She is Panicking,
PUSH IN on her

13

CUT TO PUSH IN
on her POV of Sign in road

14

CUT BACK to Driver,
she swerves to avoid

15

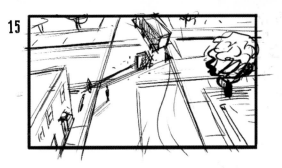

CUT TO HIGH OVERHEAD
TRUCK SWERVES around sign
head to opposite side of the road...

16A

CUT TO
Saint of Killers
PUSH IN on him, as he becomes

16B

CONT
awash in the HEADLIGHTS of the TRUCK

17A

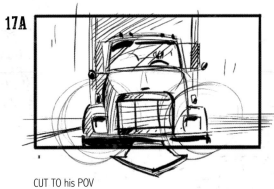

CUT TO his POV
TRUCK comes straight at him

17B

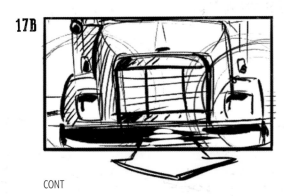

CONT

18A

CUT TO
on Saint in profile, as the TRUCK blasts in and...

18B

CONT
TRUCK hits Saint of Killers
keeps going

18C

CONT
CAM PAN Truck as it slams into a TREE

19A

CUT TO
MED on JESSE, as he watches, stunned

19B

CONT
Jesse goes to investigate

20

CUT TO
His POV, Driver stumbles out and staggers away

21A

CUT BACK to JESSE,
continues forward, Driver staggers past him

21B

CONT
Jesse walks into tight CU

22A

CUT TO Jesse POV
ARM of Saint, protrudes from wreckage
CAM MOVES DOWN

22B

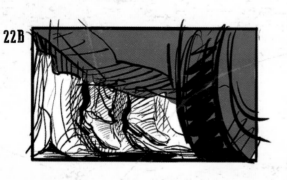

CONT
REVEALS Saint's feet dangling just above the ground, as he is
    pinned to tree

23A

CUT BACK to JESSE
(no one survives that crash)

23B

CONT
Jesse turns to head back to Motel

24A

CUT TO WIDE
on Jesse, walking away from wreck

24B

CONT
CAM Around him revealing all the conventioneer gun guys
    coming out of the MOTEL to see what's going on

25A

CUT TO
MED on the guys, with their guns,
Cassidy is among them, all are in robes and PJs

25B

CONT
Cassidy comes to CAM out of the crowd

26

CUT BACK TO JESSE
he comes to CAM, as WRECKAGE starts to move, backwards
    a bit, metal creaks and groans

27A

CUT TO REVERSE angle,
as Jesse turns to look

28A

CUT TO his clean POV
Truck is shuddering backwards from the tree
(INTERCUT PUSH IN on this with PUSH IN on JESSE REACT)

27B

CUT TO CU JESSE,
he watches intently
CAM PUSHING IN

28B

INTERCUT with wreck moving and SAINT starts to emerge

27C

CUT BACK TO PUSH IN on JESSE TO CU

28C

CUT BACK TO SAINT,
Marching out of wreck

29

CUT TO CU Saint,
he adjusts his hat a bit

27D

CUT BACK to Jesse,
he is stunned. What IS PLAN B?

27E

CONT
He looks over his shoulder, back to gun guys,
(here is Plan B)

27F

CONT He turns back to face Saint
WoG to Gun Guys: "STOP HIM"
He points to Saint of Killers

29

CUT TO
Tracking shot of Gun Guys, looking shocked by their
bodies' reaction, loading guns, formed a firing line

30A

CUT TO High shot down the firing line, muzzles flash,
CAM Tracks down the line

31

CUT TO on the Saint of Killers, he is riddled with bullets,
jerking with the impact like a puppet
PUSH IN

30B

CUT BACK to firing line
at the end of the line is a grenade launching gun,

32A

CUT TO Over the firing line
we see the grenade fly towards the Saint of Killers

32B

CONT
He is HIT, it explodes

33

CUT TO Gun Guys
they react to explosion

34

CUT TO their POV,
Dust and smoke where the Saint once was

35

CUT TO Jesse and Cassidy, they are now over to the side,
no longer in front of the firing line
PAN OFF them to

36A

CONT
The Gun Guys, they whoop and holler. Success!
CAM TRACK down the line of guys,

36B

CONT
on last guy, foreground, as he turns to see...

37

CUT TO POV of the smoke cloud as the Saint of Killers
emerges

38A

CUT TO MED SHOT on Saint

38B

CONT
ON Saint of Killers as he flexes his torso,
BULLETS all pop out of his body and

39

CUT TO
Shot on the ground at his feet, slugs drop into frame and
bounce around, piling up around his boots

40

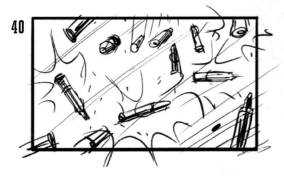

ALT SHOT of slugs hitting CAM
(as though we can see up through the ground)

41

CUT BACK to Jesse and Cassidy,
they react to this

42A

CUT TO
ANGLE ON GUN, at the side of the Saint of Killers
(Gun is pointing to the ground)

42B

CONT
CAM HOLD ON GUN,
As it is raised up

42B

CONT
To parallel to the ground, and we see the other gun in the
background, lined up

43A

CUT TO
Jesse pushing in

43B

CONT
He turns in the Tight CU
PAN OFF his look...

43C

CONT
CAM PAN TO adjacent line of Gun Guys, they are furiously
trying to reload (MUSKET guy at the end of the line)

44

CUT BACK to Jesse,
he turns back

45A

CUT TO Jesse's POV
TIGHT on Saint, pulling out as he

45B

CONT
raises his guns

46

CUT BACK TO JESSE
He yells RU...is drowned out by report
BOOM!

47

CUT BACK to Saint
Guns blazing

48A

CUT to Firing line, as the guys are being cut down
TRACK ALONG guys, and PAN off them

48B

CONT
PAN to pick up Jesse and Cassidy as they take cover nearby
(dumpster near motel?)

49

CUT TO Jesse, pushing in
He yells RUN again, louder

50

CUT TO his POV of guys, some hear and run, others are
down, others still trying to stop Saint of Killers

51A

CUT TO TWO SHOT
Jesse and Cassidy,
Dialogue as Jesse tries to run back, Cassidy stops him,

51B

PUSH IN on them,
dialogue continues,

51C

CONT PUSH IN, Landing in Cassidy:

"Where's Tulip?"

51D

CONT
CAM PAN TO JESSE, he Turns to look towards Motel
(where IS she?)

52A

CUT TO BLACK

52B

CONT
CAM MOVE UP off back of TV SET,
reveal Tulip, glued to set, enter Jesse in background
"You hear that? We gotta go!"

52C

CONT Tulip: "Look..."
now Jesse is glued too
Cassidy enters in background: "We gotta go! What is it?"

52D

CONT
Jesse: "Look..."
Cassidy is glued.

53A

CUT TO PUSH IN on TV SET,
We see explosion, with Banner scroll

53B

CONT (NO SOUND, just banners)
"Annville Apocalypse...Survivors highly unlikely...Methane
    Plant confirmed as cause..." etc.

54

CUT TO PUSH in on our Heroes

IN MEMORIAM MONTAGE

Montage of Characters from season 1,
"in memorium" clips of existing footage

55A

(FADE?) back to TV SCREEN
Dust and smoke is clearing,
TOWN is Annihilated

55B

CONT
BLAM!
bullet blasts through TV, shattering screen

56A

CUT BACK TO the TRIO,
they react...

56B

CONT
They snap out of it, and grab their stuff and head out

57

CUT TO Hallway, MOTEL
CAM Follow as they head to EXIT sign pointing to adjoining
hallway

58A

CUT TO REV angle,
CAM Leads them

58B

CONT OR CUT (PAN to View down hallway/cut to POV)
We see Saint of Killers at opposite end of hall, shooting
into a room (he has come into building through exit)

59

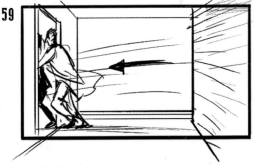

CUT TO REV Angle
Tulip, Jesse, Cassidy keep going straight into Vending
Machine room

60

CUT TO REV Angle, down the hall, as Saint of Killers moves
towards CAM, kicking in doors and shooting people in
the rooms

61A

CUT TO STEADY CAM inside Snack Room,
On the TRIO, huddled against wall inside door,
CAM DOES A FULL ROTATION of the room

61B

Passing the COLD DRINKS machine,

61C

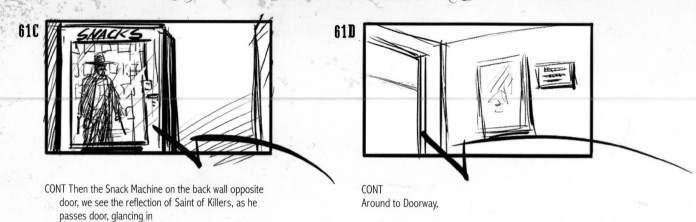

CONT Then the Snack Machine on the back wall opposite
door, we see the reflection of Saint of Killers, as he
passes door, glancing in

61D

CONT
Around to Doorway,

61E

CONT
Rotating shot on Doorway, Saint is moving off down
hallway, looking in rooms

62A

(CONT OR CUT) onto Cassidy, Tulip and Jesse
T: "Genesis, I think now is an ok time..."
J: "Tried. Doesn't work."

62B

CAM PAN to show Cassidy, trying to open window,
it's STUCK

62C

CONT
Tulips whips out a pocket knife or tool of some kind,
goes to work on the window

62D

CONT
A SOUND by the door, they look over

63A

CUT TO ANGLE (not really a POV)
on Conventioneer, with one arm blown off, entering

63B

CAM PAN him to the COLD DRINK machine,
he feeds in his dollar
(the gang is behind him, staring)

64

CUT TO their POV, with other machine in background, with
reflection of SOK still heading away down hall
Conventioneer: "Hey! I pressed ROOT BEER!"

65

CUT BACK TO OVER HIM,
as they try to shush him,
Dialogue covered in these shots

66

CUT BACK to Conventioneer
"I pressed root beer not ginger ale!"

67

CUT TO OVER HIM starts to pound machine
I WANT ROOT BEER
Jesse with WoG: (low whisper) "BE QUIET"

68A

CUT TO PUSH IN ON ECU of EAR of Saint of Killers
(he can hear the WoG)

68B

CONT
hold on him, as he turns
his eyes squint

69A

CUT TO Conventioneer:
(Quietly) "I want Root Beer."
CAM PUSH PAST HIM

69 B

CONT
To Reflection in Machine behind
Saint is heading back towards them

70

CUT TO CU Jesse react to this
PUSH IN

71A

CUT TO Behind Saint of Killers
CAM FOLLOW HIM

71B

CONT
through door of Snack Room, rounds corner to see EMPTY
room save the Conventioneer

72

CUT TO low angle CU on Saint
He sees

73A

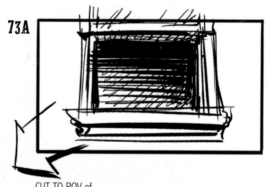

CUT TO POV of
OPEN WINDOW
CAM move down to...

73B

CONT
CAM to Conventioneer
"Got any quarters?"

74A

CUT TO Angle on DRINK MACHINE,
Saint slams Conventioneer into the machine

CAM TILT down to see
QUARTERS pouring out of the change return slot

CUT TO EXTERIOR MOTEL
HIGH and WIDE, Caution light swings in the foreground,
CHEVELLE speeds away into the distance

75B

CAM DOWN, Over Saint, watching them disappear into the
distance

75C

CONT
CAM comes around
PUSHING IN on Saint, he grits his teeth

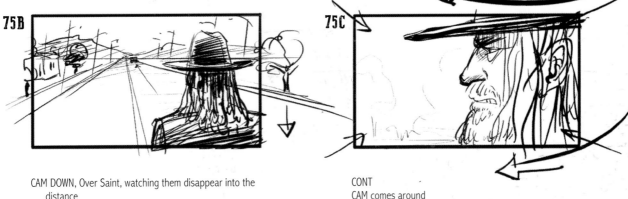

THE SAINT IMPRISONED

The Saint cannot be killed, but Jesse concocts a clever plan to neutralize his enemy for good. It's a plan tinged with cruelty: to lock a man who cannot die up in a metal prison and send him to the bottom of a swamp. The Saint goes from one Hell, to another.

Season Two, Episode Twelve: Directed by Michael Slovis. Storyboards by Paulo DeFreitas Jr

FROM BLACK…

ARMORED TRUCK DESCENDS AWAY FROM CAMERA…

TO THE DEPTHS OF THE SWAMP

AND DISAPPEARS INTO DARKNESS

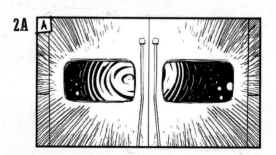

(POV FROM INT. TRUCK WINDOW)
LIGHT FROM SURFACE IS VISIBLE THROUGH WATER AS
TRUCK DESCENDS INTO SWAMP

2B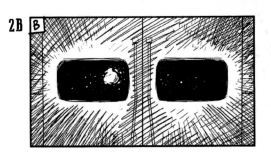

LIGHT MOVES AWAY FROM WINDOW AS TRUCK DESCENDS
DEEPER INTO SWAMP

2C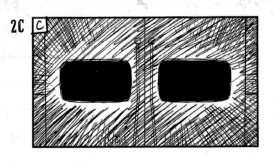

LIGHT COMPLETELY VANISHES

3A

TRUCK DESCENDS INTO DARKNESS…

3B

FRONT HITS BOTTOM…

3C

THEN THE REAR

4A

(SAINT OF KILLERS POV FROM INT. TRUCK WINDOW)
CAMERAS BY RIGHT WINDOW
AS LIGHT REVEALS THE SHADOW OF A DIVER

4B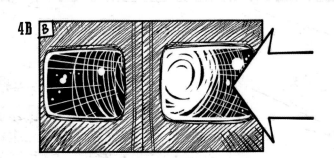

LIGHT TURNS TO CAMERA AS CAMERA MOVES FROM RIGHT TO
LEFT WINDOW

4C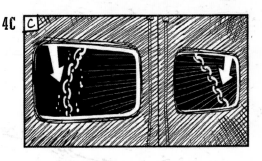

CHAINS DROP OUTSIDE WINDOWS

5A

(LOW ANGLE)
AS SAINT OF KILLERS LOOKS OUT THE WINDOW

5B

TRUCK IS PULLED OUT OF SWAMP AND SAINT SLIDES
BACKWARDS TOWARDS THE CAB

5C

LIGHT FLOODS INTO WINDOW

ACKNOWLEDGMENTS

Sony Pictures Television and Titan Books would like to thank the following people for making this book possible:

Seth Rogen, Evan Goldberg, Sam Catlin, Garth Ennis, Dominic Cooper, Ruth Negga, Joseph Gilgun, Graham McTavish, Ian Coletti, Pip Torrens, Julie Ann Emery, Malcolm Barrett, Tom Brooke, Amy Hill, David Blass, Christopher Lucero, Jessica Nubel, Chris Van Amburg, Lauren Townsend, Scott Gorenstein, Allison Begalman, Cindy Irwin and Misara Shao.